BIBLICAL MARRIAGE

In his book, *Biblical Marriage,* John-William Noble provides the church with a concise and accessible addition to Christian marriage literature. It is not only theologically robust, but it is pastoral and practically wise: even using examples from Pastor Noble's own marriage to teach the reader. This is an excellent pew-level resource which should be widely read. Buy it!

—GAVIN PEACOCK, Associate Pastor, Calvary Grace Church, Calgary, Director of International Outreach for CBMW, author, former professional footballer and BBC Sport broadcaster

Throughout the years, so many unhelpful books have been written on marriage that fail to demonstrate the beauty of a man and woman typifying Christ and his church. John-William Noble has served the church well by providing a work that does just that. The title, *Biblical Marriage,* properly defines this excellent work. Thoroughly biblical and theologically sound, Noble paints the portrait of a marriage, not as culture defines it, but as Scripture commands it.

—DUSTIN BENGE, Provost and Professor of Church History, Union School of Theology, Bridgend, Wales

Marriage books that are God-centred, gospel-saturated, and biblically driven are rare in a market chock-full of tomes on relationships. John-William Noble's new book, *Biblical Marriage,* is a breath of fresh air in a climate not always friendly to the idea of distinctly Christian marriage. Even though the definition of marriage seems to be ever-evolving in our culture, no such evolution exists in Scripture. Marriage is a holy union between a man and a woman for a lifetime. Marriage is a great drama that tells the deeper and more wonderful story of the love of Jesus for his church. John-William Noble serves the church well in *Biblical Marriage,* a book that will land you on the certain foundation of the Bible, provide for you a vision of a Christ-exalting marriage, and offer you practical counsel that you can put to work in your marriage. Get this book, read this book, practice this book.

—RAY RHODES JR., Author of *Yours, Till Heaven: The Untold Love Story of Charles and Susie Spurgeon,* and Pastor of Grace Community Church of Dawsonville, GA

John-William's book is a refreshing addition to Christian literature on marriage. Whilst many books have been written from the point of view of psychology, there are relatively few that build principles firmly on the solid rock of the Bible's teachings. John-William does not shy away from countercultural views when they are based on Scripture, showing how the word of God can and should inform every aspect of a successful marriage.

—**LUKE JEFFERY,** Director, Onwards and Upwards Publishers

This book's opening chapter lays a firm biblical foundation, and the final chapter pleads for a biblical culture in understanding marriage. In between, the author rigorously asserts biblical principle, defining marriage as a reflection of God's covenant love in Christ. He faces the practicalities of married life with self-awareness and realism and offers wise counsel. His own experience of a cross-cultural marriage and the fact that he is a young man enhances the book's value.

—**JONATHAN BAYES,** UK Director, Carey Outreach Ministries, and Pastor, Stanton Lees Chapel, Derbyshire, United Kingdom

In this book Pastor Noble reveals an overriding concern that our marriages should glorify God, and he deals very honestly with the practical topics treated. He is very clear that even the best of marriages is a marriage between two sinners, and that biblical ideals cannot be implemented without both the grace of God and real effort on our part. This is a challenging and thought-provoking book.

—**GILBERT McADAM,** Pastor, Harbour Mission Baptist Church, Wick, Scotland

This book is worth reading as it helps to understand the biblical perspective of marriage. The time in which we are living we see the devil is distorting the truth of the Bible on marriage and its essence. Marriage was God's idea between a man and woman. God blessed the marriage between one man and woman. I do pray that this book changes lives. The writer is a true man of God who has unpacked biblical truth about marriage.

—**AMIR SHAHBAZ BHATTI,** Author of *Christian Tears of Pakistan: Falsely Accused Under Blasphemy Law 295-BC,* and Pastor, Agape Church and Mission for Pakistan

I highly recommend this book especially to single people who are planning to get married. This is not to say that married couples won't benefit from it. The wisdom and clarity of thought are on full display as John-William Noble offers practical biblical help to understand what a biblical marriage should look like.

—**SONNY SIMAK,** Pastor, Grace Church Southall, United Kingdom

Biblical Marriage is a book that accomplishes much for its size. It not only outlines the biblical framework of what marriage is, but deals with a host of practical matters, including the topics of trust, sexual purity, and finances. John-William Noble has, therefore, written a tremendously helpful book. He does not stop at faithfully presenting the biblical teaching on marriage but goes on to faithfully apply it to everyday life. And yet none of this was a surprise to me. *Biblical Marriage* is simply consistent with what I know about its author: a sinner saved by grace, who seeks to love God and neighbour, and who seeks to be scriptural in all of life. I very gladly recommend this volume to all who are married, and to those who are pursuing marriage in the future.

—**DANIEL FUNKE,** Pastor, Grace Baptist Church Govan, Glasgow, Scotland

Marriage is at the heart of God's vision for family life, so where better to seek enlightenment on the topic than in God's word? That's exactly what John-William Noble does. From the theological foundations to day-to-day applications, we are presented with God's relational wisdom, in this concise, straight-talking, and warm little book.

—**RICHARD LUCAS,** Leader of The Scottish Family Party, Glasgow, Scotland

BIBLICAL MARRIAGE

Two Sinners and a Gracious God

John-William Noble

RESOURCE *Publications* · Eugene, Oregon

Wipf & Stock
An Imprint of Wipf and Stock Publishers
199 W. 8th Ave., Suite 3
Eugene, OR 97401
www.wipfandstock.com

Paperback ISBN: 978-1-7252-8763-1
Hardcover ISBN: 978-1-7252-8762-4
eBook ISBN: 978-1-7252-8764-8

Manufactured in the U.S.A.

To Binglin Luo Noble
my beautiful bride, my loving wife,
of all excellent women you surpass them all.

* * *

All Glory be to our God
through Christ Jesus our Lord.
Amen.

Special thanks go to:
John and Elizabeth Noble, my parents
who have modelled Godly marriage.

* * *

Daniel Funke, for his typesetting and editorial expertise.
Jonathan Bayes, Fraser Munro and Elizabeth Noble (mum)
for proofreading (and thereby improving!) this book.
And Gavin Peacock for kindly writing a Biblical foreword.

CONTENTS

FOREWORD

IT'S FAIR TO say that our modern world is in the midst of sexual confusion and immorality, especially in the area of marriage. Yet to understand marriage you have to go to a different source than the newspapers, magazines or TV. To appreciate the grand design of God for holy matrimony, you have to go to the Holy Scriptures. This was Jesus' own default position. In Matthew 19 the Pharisees are trying to trap Jesus whilst asking a question on marriage and divorce. So, Jesus answers,

> Have you not read that he who created them from the beginning made them male and female, and said, 'Therefore a man shall leave his father and his mother and hold fast to his wife, and the two shall become one flesh'? So they are no longer two but one flesh. What therefore God has joined together, let not man separate. (Matthew 19:4-6)

Drawing from Genesis 1:27 and 2:24, Jesus appeals to God's Word at creation to define marriage. The Apostle Paul affirms this thinking in Ephesians 5 when he quotes Genesis 2:24 and says that marriage from creation is a picture of the gospel (Ephesians 5:31-32). Finally, the Apostle John records a heavenly vision of the 'Marriage Supper of the Lamb' after the Jesus, the Bridegroom, comes to take his Bride, the Church, to himself forever (Revelation 19:6-9). So, we could say that marriage at creation is a picture of God's love in redemption that points us all the way to consummation. Therefore, although marriage is not the gospel it has massive theological significance connected to the gospel. This means that marriage is profoundly doctrinal. And men and women as husbands and wives are used to display these tremendous universal realities. And we must also remember that marriage is the foundation of the family and society, as children become the fruit of the union of husband and wife and are to be trained in the Lord (Ephesians 6:1-4).

Yet marriage is under attack in our culture in a way not quite seen before. It is being redefined and even the very question of whether there is such a thing as manhood and womanhood, fixed binary sexes, is being assaulted. In addition to cultural attack, marriage is being undervalued in the church where young men and women are not being trained to aim for it and not being taught how to be a husband or wife.

Therefore, we are at a time when we need to return to basics, to the sources—ad fontes—and to the sufficiency of the Scriptures to define who we are, what marriage is and what it looks like looks like on the ground. This is why I am delighted that John-William Noble has written a book entitled *Biblical Marriage*. Page after page is filled with Biblical foundations and sound exegesis. And with chapters on blame, trust, lust, money and parenting, the author offers practical and pastoral wisdom for the reader to apply to his or her life and relationship with their spouse. Sin and grace is the enduring theme.

Above all, this book honours Jesus Christ, as Pastor Noble consistently makes effortless and natural connections to the gospel. In the end the reader is left with an accessible book that shows how the gospel that saves a sinful husband and wife is the gospel they are called to picture in their marriage, and the gospel love they show when they forgive and forbear is the glue which holds them together. I pray this book encourages many marriages and also encourages many to marry.

Gavin Peacock
August 2020

INTRODUCTION

'I'm single, so it doesn't relate to me!'
I HAVE LOST count of the number of times I have heard a preacher or a Christian writer introduce the topic of marriage, or even relationships, in the following (sort of) way:

> Ok brothers and sisters, today we are going to begin studying the topic of marriage. Now even if you are not married, if you want to get married one day then this series will be helpful for you. And if you don't want to get married, then you will be better equipped to pray for and support your married friends.

This type of introduction is not necessarily wrong, but it could be compared to my focus being on my need to sleep to avoid eye bags. The reasoning is sound, but it is not the principle reason, and such an emphasis would miss the point of the action. The gift of marriage is a gift given to us by God for God. Yet, within Christian circles, it has become so very evidently self-serving in relation to our life as a Christian. However, what needs to be made clear is that the beauty of marriage is first and foremost a beauty that every believer can explore and rejoice in because of what it actually is. This is something that will be explored in the first chapter, which unpacks what the Scriptures say about 'Biblical marriage'. The trap that many could then fall into in reading such a book is to think, 'OK, there is some Bible teaching, but what I really want to know is how to get a wife or husband, or how to improve my marriage'. These are legitimate practical issues but they are in no way detached from the foundation and application of the saving truth of the Gospel. This is why the absolutely fundamental point that must be stressed is that our understanding of anything in Scripture is through the lens of the cross and that the Christian's understanding of anything in life is based on Scripture.

Therefore one might ask: Why is marriage an important topic for every Christian, regardless of their relationship status? It is because marriage has been instituted by God (Matthew 19:6) for His Glory and because it is a picture of a man and woman in a covenant relationship that points us to Christ's relationship with His church, His bride, whom He has rescued and is now perfecting for the banquet feast of heaven. Undoubtedly this is the most significant reason for studying this topic and as an outworking of this it then becomes very beneficial to unpack the practical realities of marriage between a man and a woman in order to glorify the Name of our Lord. We will not and we cannot 'move past' this reality when studying this topic and I thank the Lord for that truth because this is the basis and blessing of what a marriage is.

'Don't write this book'
I began writing part of the material for this book as a blog, which I intended to be practical advice for young Christians thinking about or in relationships. However, I soon realised that this blog was already surpassing any reasonable word count for a 'readable' blog and so things began to expand. As the material began to take shape however, I was advised not to write this book. As a relatively young man whose experience of marriage in years is still very much in single digits, I am writing as one who is very much learning the importance of growing in a marriage rooted in Scripture. It was suggested that writing about something of which I had comparably limited experience of was not a wise idea, and yet interestingly this was the premise for my writing. The basis for teaching on anything in Scripture must be Scripture, and the practical insight in this book is based on my contemporary

thoughts and even struggles as one who is seeking to grow in wisdom and discernment from the Lord as a married man. This is why I have sought to be very practical in giving practical examples and lessons from my own marriage.

My story

I spent a period of time serving in a church in Edinburgh at the beginning of 2013, which included leading an International fellowship. One evening, after the meeting of this fellowship had started and we were singing our opening hymn, a young Chinese woman stood next to me (I had hoped it was to stand next to the tall, handsome stranger but the lack of empty seats elsewhere was certainly a contributing factor). I could see she seemed a little lost, a newcomer clearly, and so I was being the *very calm, caring guy* in giving her my hymn book to join in the worship. It was important that this woman did not realise that my heart was beating much faster now. I had become more conscious of my every movement and the fact that I had just had my hair cut hours earlier and that it looked messy (I was later told that my old and unfashionable footwear was the biggest 'turn off' but I was blissfully unaware of this at the time). Despite my nervousness, I introduced myself to this woman, named Binglin, and we got on well. I was attracted to her and her openness to speak about the Lord and so we spent some time talking on the first evening. As the weeks passed by, we started to communicate more regularly, as well as meeting together. She was still relatively young in her spiritual journey but had a very clear and focussed desire to live her life more and more closely with her Saviour. It also became clear to me that we had significantly different cultural perspectives and expectations about relationships, given the fact that she was born and brought up in China. There are many amusing stories and anecdotes that could be unravelled at this point (some later in the book), but the most important realisation as we grew closer together was the importance of *de-emphasising* our culture. Binglin and I both so easily referred to a 'right' way of doing things on a number of topics based on what we understood from our upbringing and cultural climates in Scotland and China. This period taught me so much about how influenced we are by our culture and this included in relation to our reading of and the practical outworkings of the Christian faith. The differences in cultural perspectives proved to be a blessing as we were very focussed in coming before God's Word to develop a more intentional Biblically-driven culture in our relationship. What does this mean? It's simple, actually: In China, we do this ... In Scotland, we do that ... so, what does the Bible say? In Scripture, we should do ...

Binglin and I got engaged over half a year after we had met and got married the following year on 19th July 2014. I love and cherish her very much and am so thankful that the Lord has blessed me with such a wonderfully understanding, caring, patient and loving wife. Yet she is a sinful woman. She annoys me, she upsets me, she frustrates me. When that is weighed up against my pride, laziness, speed at which I lose my temper, the ease by which I will engage in trivial activities rather than take time to care for my wife, my selfishness, arrogance and much, much more, how great is our need of the grace of God in marriage! This is not a self-effacing list to hint that I am 'really a decent guy'. This may be the image that the world sees but in marriage you are exposed. You cannot hide your sinful desires and behaviours in the home, in a marriage. It is real and this will be drawn out thoroughly in this book.

Therefore, the title of this book becomes realistic as well as relevant. For any Christian couple who come together in marriage, this is the coming together of two saved sinners whose identity is in Christ, but they are still actively at war against sin. We live in a time in history where Christ has won the victory over sin and death, but until He returns, sin is still a rampant force and the devil is still at work. Imagine you are a patient with a life-threatening tumour in your body and the doctor successfully removes it. You are cancer free, but there is a period that follows where you are medically well but still fighting the effects of that cancer. You need to be careful, for the week after that surgery you will not go and do a bungee jump or go-kart racing with your kids! This gives an imperfect picture of where we are at now. We live in the victory of Christ, but until He returns, we are still battling the effects of that sinful nature which has been put to death.

When anyone is considering or preparing for marriage, or when someone is examining their marriage or counselling others in their marriages—Be real! Be real about who the person is that you are going to marry, and be real about who you are and then consider the inevitable issues that may arise. It is only by the restoration that my wife and I have at the cross that we can prayerfully seek to move on an upward trajectory in our marriage because we seek to actively and prayerfully wage war on the sin that can so easily crush our marriage. This is what we must explore in this book by initially studying the Scriptures to know what the Lord says about marriage and how this then applies to a number of important practical areas within any given marriage.

HOW IMPORTANT IS
'BIBLICAL' MARRIAGE?

WHY DO CHRISTIANS want to get married in a church? Isn't it just a bit of paper? Why one man and one woman?
Western society today is a very inquisitive and challenging one where the emphasis on the rights, the freedom of choice of the individual drives popular, public consensus. Further still, the very laws of our land and definitions of terms such as marriage have been questioned, ridiculed and changed. Marriage itself is now recognised as a legal or formal union between any two people as opposed to being between one man and one woman. Therefore, when we come to ask a question—How important is 'Biblical marriage'?—we can see why this is a very necessary question for Christians in such a context. We also learn that the culture has already given a clear answer: 'Not very!'

However, the necessity of the question lies simply in the fact that the Bible is the inspired Word of God (2 Timothy 3:16) and that marriage is designed by God, it is defined by God and it is for the purpose of the Glory of God. Therefore, it is the Scriptures that we must unashamedly and desperately cleave to in our desire to know what marriage is and its great importance according to the Sovereign purpose of the Lord.

God created … male and female

In order to consider how important Biblical marriage is, we ought to explore what Biblical marriage is. To do this, we go to the Scriptures and we begin at the very beginning in the book of Genesis: 'So God created man in his own image, in the image of God he created him; male and female he created them' (Genesis 1:27).

This is the pinnacle of the account of God's creation in Genesis 1—The creation of mankind. There are numerous observations that can be made here, but let us draw out the two points which are very clear from verse 27. The first is that God creates man, namely humanity, in His image. Nothing else is created in the image of God, and this instantly gives weight to the argument that humanity is the unique and special creation of God. What a blessed gift that is! The second point to draw from this verse is that God creates 'man' male and female. Male and female.

Permit me to state what is obvious from the text. God is the creator. He designs humanity. It is His design, His purpose to create human beings in His image. It is also according to His Sovereign decree and purpose to create some human beings as male and some human beings as female. What is also clear is that the differences between male and female are not simply due to their physical make up! I have been informed that there is much scientific evidence indicating the prevalent differences between the male and female brain. This point must be stressed because it is emphasised at the account of creation. It also must be stressed because it is a fundamental base by which we can understand Biblical marriage.

Marriage is God's design, not man's idea

As we progress in our consideration of what Biblical marriage is, we only need to scroll our eyes to the very next Chapter of the book of Genesis. In the beginning of Scripture we have a detailed account of the creation of the world and then a specific focus upon God's purpose for creation. This involves an authority given to the man, and the responsibility of working in and maintaining God's creation (Genesis 2:15). We can infer that God created the man first by the assertion of Genesis 2:18: 'Then the Lord God said, "It is not good that the man should be alone; I will make him a helper fit for him."'

As we consider the remaining verses of Genesis 2 (vv. 19-25) we come to a crucial passage in helping us to understand Biblical marriage. This begins with an initial consideration of the differences between male and female.

What we see in verse 15 is that the man has been created before the woman and that the man has already been given a role of authority in the Garden of Eden (Genesis 2:8). This is important as we come to verse 18 and carefully unpack what this verse says and means. God's purpose for the man has been made clear in verses 15 and 18. We now see two purposes for the woman according to our verse. First, as a companion to the man. Second, as a helper.

1. Companion

The man has been given a role and work to do in the Garden of Eden. Should we conclude then that the role of the woman is simply to assist with the *practical* demands of the man's work? We should not, and verse 18 (see above) makes it clear why. The man, created perfectly, without fault and in fellowship with God in this Garden and with work to do. And yet, the Lord declares that it is not good that this man be *alone*. That is an incredible declaration. It tells us so much, none more so than that our Glorious God has made His creation to have and to be blessed with human companionship. That is not to suggest that God is any way insufficient or not enough for man, but that physically, emotionally, relationally on the earth, our being is one that is made to enjoy being together with other people (and I would add, thus enjoying the beauty and Glory of God together!).

The account that follows in the remaining verses of Genesis 2 helps us to then see the significance of companionship in marriage. When we read that no suitable 'helper' can be found for the man (Genesis 2:20), the man falls into a deep sleep (Genesis 2:21) and then God creates woman from the rib of the man (2:21). When the man sees the woman his reaction is as follows, 'This at last is bone of my bones and flesh of my flesh; she shall be called Woman, because she was taken out of Man' (Genesis 2:23).

The language used by the man here is striking! The man acknowledges the unique difference between the woman and the animals over which he has been given responsibility and rule. It would not be reading too much into the text to see the emotional delight of the man as he stands before the woman. The phrase 'this at last' is poetic language, which indicates his instant, joyful recognition of this creature that is wholly different from the animals. The significance of this companionship will be drawn out further when we look at the institution of marriage in verse 24, but we can see the delight of the man at this outcome. A companion has been found and what a companion! The beautifully formed woman!

2. Helper

The purpose of the woman is also made clear in verse 18, and again in verse 20, by the word 'helper'. Before we apply this term in the context of marriage, we should seek to carefully and clearly understand what this term means.

The original Hebrew term is *ezer* which is a phrase even used to describe God in His help to human beings in the Old Testament. Therefore, it is very clear that this is not a term used to suggest the inferiority of the woman. We have already noted that both male and female are created in the image of God (Genesis 1:27) and this term does in no way contradict this. However, it has been argued that the use of the term *ezer* means that there is no subordinate role of the woman to the man. This conclusion has often been a springboard for the theological position known as 'egalitarianism'. The term 'egalitarianism' literally means 'equal' and it argues for the equality of male and female in every way. Proponents argue that there are no distinct roles between male and female, and they point out that the term 'helper' is used to describe God's help to human beings and that He is in no way subordinate to human beings. Now it is correct to say that the term *ezer* itself does not infer a subordinate role, and so what we must seek to do is understand the context in which the term is used. We can safely conclude that the term used about God does not imply such a thing, but there are also instances in the Old Testament when the term does infer subordinate help. Therefore, it is crucial to understand the meaning and application of the term in its context. What the egalitarian position has done is to give examples of where the term has been used elsewhere (in relation to God) as a means of stating that it cannot mean subordination in Genesis 2. However, that is not transferable without further clarification of the actual meaning of the term in the passage. As we study the passage in context we then see that there is no grounding for an egalitarian position, but rather, a 'complementarian' position; namely, that men and women are created equal but with different roles that complement each other in life, in relationships including marriage.

The beautiful unique role of a woman in marriage as a 'helper' can be founded again on the Lord's declaration in verse 18. It is 'not good' that the man be alone. What does this imply? The man is incomplete, he *needs* help. However, we must realise that by the Sovereign decree of the Lord, the man has been created first, his task in working and being in charge of the Garden is already clear. There is a primary responsibility, an initial role, an authority, leadership that is given to the man. This is God's design, it is before sin has entered the world and it is beautiful.

The role of the woman in relationship to the man is one of completion and complementation. We see in Genesis 2:22 that the woman is formed from the rib of the man which is a vivid picture of a woman standing by the side of the man, for she is needed by the man (again, note Genesis 2:18). She is made equal (Genesis 1:27) and made to complement the leadership role that is given to the man according to God's design.

Is this unfair? Is it 'sexist'? Why is the woman not made in her own right as opposed to being a companion and helper for a man? The easy way to answer is to declare that it is the Sovereign purpose of the Living God. However, we can go further to emphasise that the woman is not fulfilling the man's purposes, but God's! Also, the woman is 'needed' because it is not good for the man to be alone, and the woman is equal to the man, made from the rib, not from the head to symbolise a man's ruling, or from the feet, to symbolise his trampling, but the side! The world can distort and try to redefine or change direction, but the Word of God stands forever (Isaiah 40:8) and God has made male and female equally, but differently—and that is a beautiful thing.

Genesis 2:24—Institution of Marriage

We have considered the creation of humanity, identifying the differences between male and female from Genesis 2 and this is our framework for seeing the institution of marriage in Genesis 2:24: 'Therefore a man shall leave his father and his mother and hold fast to his wife, and they shall become one flesh.'

God has created human beings to enjoy the practical, emotional and spiritual blessing of companionship—particularly in the blessed institution of marriage. There is much to unravel from this verse, none more so than identifying that this is not a 'there and then' application for the man and woman in the Garden of Eden, but rather a more general application for a man and woman coming together in marriage. The book of Genesis has been written by Moses, centuries later, inspired by the Living God, and the Lord is giving a broader framework for understanding something that God has beautifully designed and instituted before sin has entered the world!

This verse ultimately points to a physical and emotional coming together of a man and woman, which will first take place between the man and woman in the Garden of Eden. However, let's draw out the details:

1. A man leaves his parents
2. Holds fast to his wife
3. They become 'one flesh'

1. A man leaves his parents

It is incredible to see the first reference to a parent-child relationship and this further establishes the importance of relationships between human beings. The Lord's design involves an individual being born of a father and mother and this creates a special bond and relationship in which a child ought to be brought up in love and discipline to know the Lord. This is emphasised in 2:24 because leaving your parents would not be stressed with such significance here if it was not important. And yet, the command is that a man 'leaves' his parents. Why? Is this about a 'coming of age' where you no longer depend on your parents? It is certainly true to say that the dynamics of your relationship with your parents change as you grow up, but the significance here is more on the greater importance of another relationship. The relationship between a husband and a wife. We know this must be the case because of what has taken place in the Garden of Eden. The Lord has provided a woman for the man in order that they can be together in marriage, which is the primary relationship in God's design of humanity. The emphasis of a man leaving his parents is crucial because he goes from a position of submission to parental authority to headship in a marriage, and the wife goes from a position of submission to her parents to submission to her husband.

2. Holds fast to his wife

The following clause is therefore crucial. A man leaves his parents and 'holds fast' to his wife. What does that mean? The NIV translates this term as 'united', which means that a man and a woman come together. The KJV uses the words 'leave' and 'cleave', namely that the man leaves his parents and cleaves to his wife. Therefore, a man is to be the husband of one wife, not many wives, one wife, and this is a relationship of permanence.

3. They become 'one flesh'

The Lord Jesus quotes this verse in Matthew 19:5 and it is interesting to note what the Lord Jesus says following this:

7

'Therefore a man shall leave his father and his mother and hold fast to his wife, and the two shall become one flesh' ... So they are no longer two but one flesh. What therefore God has joined together, let not man separate (Matthew 19:5-6).

The Lord Jesus' words are infinitely perfect and render any attempts I make to explain this verse in Genesis redundant. Notice what Jesus draws out regarding the man and woman becoming 'one flesh', they are 'no longer two'. What does that *not* mean first of all? It does not mean that a man and woman in marriage are no longer physically two individual human beings. It also does not mean that a man and a woman in marriage are no longer able to independently do and think for themselves. So what does it mean? It means that in the eyes of the Living God, when a man and a woman come together in marriage, they come together in a life-long commitment before Him and in His name (Malachi 2:14-16)! That's a pretty big deal!

The earthly permanence of this relationship is incomparable to anything else. Children leave their parents' home, friends can come and go, but a marriage is a life-long commitment, literally where two people cleave together, they come together as 'one'. This must be stressed as a covenant relationship before God because this is the foundation by which a marriage will survive (this is the backbone of many practical applications in later chapters). A couple may be greatly attracted to each other, passionately in love with each other, taking romance to all new heights, but this is not the substance of this 'one flesh' description in Genesis 2:24. When Jesus says in Matthew 19:6 that this is what God has joined together, this is deliberate. As great as it would be for a couple to be romantically and lovingly 'on fire' every day of their lives, this is not only unrealistic, but it is also a sidetrack from the main issue—God. In marriage, a husband and a wife come together, literally 'forsaking all others' in any romantic, physical and even emotional ways.

A married couple become 'one flesh' because they are now seen as 'one' in the eyes of God. This means:

- A couple can and should consummate their marriage physically. Sexual intercourse is a beautiful expression of the

love and togetherness of a man and woman in marriage.
This is not an 'optional extra' (see 1 Corinthians 6:12-7:7),
but a means by which a couple can experience that unique
togetherness as 'one flesh'. This is also the means by which
man and woman can 'be fruitful and multiply'.

- A couple are emotionally invested in each other's lives. The
  Lord blessed the man with a helper who is also a companion, for the chief end of God's Glory, and this is the purpose of man's role in leadership and the woman's role as his
  helpmate. We are relational beings and the closeness and
  intimacy of an emotional relationship between a husband
  and a wife is a special, precious thing!

- A couple are spiritually united. This cannot be emphasised
  enough. God puts a man and a woman together. That is
  not a 'take it or leave it' type of relationship. That is not an
  'if it's going well, then I'll stick it out' type of relationship.
  That is a spiritually binding relationship, which is why
  it is called a 'covenant', namely a sworn oath, between a
  man and a woman in the presence of the Living God! In
  this, every marriage therefore proclaims the Glory of God,
  delighting in the Sovereignty of God in His purpose for
  marriage and this is what centrally makes this a life-long,
  binding, 'one flesh' commitment.

Pointing to the Gospel

In the Garden of Eden, we see that the man and woman are
naked and feel no shame (Genesis 2:25) but this perfect union
is soon ruined by man's disobedience against the Living God
in Genesis 3, thus leading to sin entering the world. As a result
of sin entering the world, man is now fallen in sin and faces
the reality of death and condemnation (Romans 5:12). Man is
no longer 'perfect' in God's image, for that perfect intimacy is
broken, and man is now in rebellion against God because of
sin. The consequence of man's rebellion in sin is not simply an
earthly death, but eternal punishment in hell (2 Thessalonians
1:5-10, Revelation 20:11-15).

Therefore, we give all the praise, honour and Glory to God for He has made the way of salvation. 'Jesus said to him, "I am the way, and the truth, and the life. No one comes to the Father except through me"' (John 14:6).

This is the beauty of the Gospel! Man cannot make himself right with God. We are sinful by birth (Psalm 51:5) and we continuously think, say and do things against God! The justice of God must punish sin. However, at the cross, the justice of God comes together with the mercy of God in an inseparable embrace because it is at the cross where God's own Son, Jesus Christ, who is both fully God and fully man, took the punishment for all God's elect, namely he or she who repents of their sins and believes in Jesus Christ as Lord and Saviour of their lives. This is why the Lord Jesus says that nobody comes to the Father except through Him (see above). It is only by the blood of Jesus, literally washing away the sins of a repentant sinner, that one can truly be forgiven and made right before the Living God. This is the Gospel. This is why Jesus came. He came to die on the cross for fallen sinners, and three days later rise from the dead, victorious over sin and death and thus ascend to be with the Father in Glory. This is the promised reality that awaits for every forgiven sinner, who is now cleansed by Christ's precious blood, and therefore justified before the Living God.

We therefore need to turn to Ephesians 5 to see that Biblical marriage is found at the very heart of Christianity and the relationship that follows, namely, the relationship between Christ and His chosen people, saved by grace, the church.

In Ephesians 5, the picture of a husband's relationship to his wife is compared to the picture of the relationship between our Saviour Jesus Christ and His unworthy bride, the church. In the context of a marriage relationship, the man's role to the wife is comparable to Christ's to the church, and likewise, the wife's role is comparable to that of the church. Therefore, it is vitally important to spend time considering the rich and weighty doctrine of Ephesians 5 to unravel this 'profound mystery'.

Filled with the Spirit, Reverence for Christ

The teaching on marriage and the comparisons between a husband and wife's relationship and that between Christ and His church in Ephesians 5 can be established and understood most effectively with a clear view of the context in which the Apostle writes. This is why we begin by referring to the command in Ephesians 5:18, 'be filled with the Spirit ...'

Notice that this is a command. The Christian is commanded to be 'filled with the Spirit'. The previous verses give warning to how one is to live and various dangers of living lives that are unwise or foolish such as drunkenness in verse 18. Therefore, the remedy is clear and profound, namely to be filled with the Spirit. We can go to great lengths to see in Scripture the mighty way by which the Holy Spirit is at work in our spiritual growth, and here we have a focus upon what we are to do as followers of Christ. In the contrast with drunkenness, an individual may fill his body with alcohol and become drunk. As we come before the Lord in prayer, read Scripture, meditate on the greatness and beauty of our Saviour, we are giving our hearts to the Lord, we are seeking and desiring Him as our greatest treasure and thus we open ourselves to the Holy Spirit who fills us richly. This must be stressed as being our day-to-day life of sanctification and not as some 'one off' supernatural experience. Every day the Holy Spirit is supernaturally at work in us, putting to death the deeds of the flesh and making us more like Christ.

This emphasis on verse 18 becomes the base by which a believer can talk and sing (verse 19), give thanks (verse 20) and submit (verse 21) out of reverence for Christ. And it is the teaching on submission in verse 21 that becomes the base of teaching on three areas of practical submission in the subsequent verses:

- wives submitting to husbands (5:22-33)
- children submitting to parents (6:1-4)
- slaves submitting to masters (6:5-9)

We will devote our attention to the first point as we unpack the glorious complexity of marriage drawn out in the remainder of Chapter 5. However, understanding verse 21 is the essential backbone of this, 'submitting to one another out of reverence for Christ.'

For the Christian who is 'filled with the Spirit', the object of his affection, the desire of his heart is now Christ. Therefore, we have a practical application of this, which is submitting to one another. As we are going to consider in the subsequent verses, the blood of Christ has secured a people, the church, and that people is Christ's body, united by His blood. Therefore, we are not vying for position or status. We are united by the desire to magnify the Glorious Saviour, Jesus Christ.

In practical terms, the Christian can now be motivated, not out of some religious duty, but out of a desire for the Living God as one 'filled with the Spirit', to seek to submit to others in service. This creates a willingness to give up time and money, to use up energy to serve the brother or sister in need. We have in the Living Head, Jesus Christ, the utmost glorious example. The Lord Jesus Christ came to this earth in all humility with a towel wrapped round His waist (John 13:4) to wash His disciples' feet. For Christ came not to be served, but to serve (Mark 10:45). He did this for our salvation, and thus as *the* example in our sanctification. We submit to each other because He has modelled it, because He has served us and He calls us to do likewise. This is why our submission is done 'out of fear of Christ' (the most literal translation). Our 'fear' is built upon the realisation that He is so mighty, so Glorious, so powerful, He is the judge, the authority, His power is mighty! We are afraid to be anywhere but in His presence and seeking to please and exalt Him. We thus submit to one another because the love that Christ has poured out upon us now fills us with a deepening love for Him and for each other. And the way that we relate to each other and our roles in life are built upon a focus upon the Lord Jesus Christ and the Sovereign purpose of the Living God. This is the premise by which the Apostle Paul goes on to write about a man and woman's relationship in marriage.

Submission

As we focus our attention upon the specific instructions given to wives and husbands regarding marriage, this will ultimately give significantly greater depth to the answer to our question of the importance of Biblical marriage. However, the initial instruction given to women regarding submission is in its context built upon the framework of the previous verse, mutual submission to Christ. A wife's submission to her husband is given as a particular example of submission in an earthly relationship ultimately for the sake of Jesus Christ. Therefore, the conclusion, the reason for a wife's submission to her husband is clearly articulated at the end of verse 21 and now in verse 22, 'Wives, submit to your own husbands, as to the Lord.'

Now some may ask, as many do (even within the church): Why? Mutual submission 'out of reverence for Christ' makes sense. However, why are there such specific commands in marriage? And why are wives submitting to husbands and not the other way around?

It is absolutely imperative that we establish our base for living and understanding Christianity, which is that the Bible is the infallible, perfectly inspired revealed Word of God (2 Timothy 3:16). Therefore, there is no error or mistake in the Scriptures, nothing that should be removed or changed or ignored and this means that Ephesians 5:22 is Scriptural truth and is to be obeyed. In addition to this, it is important that we seek the Spirit's guidance in how we accurately interpret seemingly difficult passages in Scripture.

The context of this verse has already been established and a wider consideration of what the Scriptures teach about marriage and male and female relationships can also provide extra insight in helping to understand this verse. In Genesis, we read about the institution of marriage prior to the fall of man. At this time, God created the man first and then created the woman from the rib of the man. This is God's designed order and, as we have already considered, this is a beautiful design. The woman was made to be a companion and helper of the man to complement him in the work that the Lord had tasked him to do in the Garden of Eden. This model, this order, as the design of God in the relationships men and women are to enjoy in marriage, is now being gloriously unpacked in Paul's teaching to the Ephesians in Chapter 5. The teaching of a wife's submission to her husband can therefore in no way be considered chauvinistic or degrading to women on the basis of Scripture as there is no Scriptural base for the notion that women are deemed inferior or 'slaves' to men. There is, nonetheless, order and structure in relationships with the Lord. We see this even in the Living and Triune God where the Son does the Will of the Father (John 6:38, 14:31) and where the Spirit comes to Glorify Christ (John 16:14). Almighty God is One God in three persons, in perfect fellowship, and yet we see order in their relationship. In addition, there is teaching in Scripture regarding submitting to authorities (Romans 13:1) and here in Ephesians 5-6 we have three relational examples of order and structure in relationships.

In Ephesians 5:22, a wife's submission to her husband 'as to the Lord' maintains the pattern of verse 21 which is joyful submission motivated and driven by the Lord Jesus Christ. This is made even clearer by the following verse: 'For the husband is the head of the wife even as Christ is the head of the church, his body, and is himself its Saviour' (Ephesians 5:23).

A wife submits to her husband 'as to the Lord' because her husband is the head. We see that this is the design and order of the Lord's creation when He created male then female, but a glorious picture is now being painted in the marriage relationship of a husband and a wife! We read here that a husband's headship over his wife is comparable to Christ's headship over the church, which is His body. Now we begin to see the glorious picture of a wife's Biblical submission!

The beautiful design of the Lord in the coming together of a man and woman in marriage from Genesis 2:24 has been smashed as a result of the fall of man. A man's authority over his wife and his wife's role in helping and complementing her husband has been greatly distorted and ruined because of sin. In our sinful world, a man's fallen state often leads to vile abuse or indifferent laziness and a woman's fallen state often leads to manipulation or domination over men. This is not the design of the Lord and we can give praise to God that in the sending of the Lord Jesus Christ He has come to redeem a people to Himself, namely the church. In Christ, every one of His people has *the* perfect Saviour, the absolutely glorious 'head' over His people, the church. To be clear, the translated word for 'head' comes from the Greek word *kephale*, which carries the connotation of supremacy and order. This is a picture we see modelled perfectly in Christ's relationship with His church because of Christ. In Ephesians 5:23, a husband's headship to his wife is to be like that of Christ to the church. Similarly, a wife's submission is to be like that of the church to Christ. Therefore, what we see in the teaching on headship and submission is a safeguard and framework for marriage as God intended it!

This teaching gives guidelines to couples in knowing how to relate to each other according to the original design of the Lord, which, though distorted by the fall, has been restored by the saving blood of Christ. For in Christ Jesus, we have the perfect model of headship which a fallen man seeks to follow. Similarly, in Christ Jesus, we have the model of the submission of the church to Christ in faith which a wife should follow. As we have identified, the world has distorted how men and women should relate together and this is why this teaching is therefore so crucial. Every marriage relationship consists of two broken sinners living in a sinful world that has distorted views about manhood, womanhood and how men and women should relate together in marriage. It is only in Jesus Christ rescuing and restoring His chosen people, the church, that we are made right by God and where marriage relationships can be lived out according to the will and purpose of God. A sinful man is not a suitable 'head' and a sinful woman cannot rightly 'submit' unless they have first submitted to Christ (verse 21) and seek to then model the relationship between Christ and the church in the covenant relationship of marriage. This is very much a battle, and there is so much to unravel in this book regarding the battles that two sinners face in marriage.

However, the victory is in Jesus Christ, the hope is in Jesus Christ, the strength is in Jesus Christ. Therefore, wives can submit to their husbands.

What then does submission look like for a Christian wife? In order to answer this question more thoroughly, let us observe the end of verse 23 regarding a husband's headship being like that of Christ to the church, 'of which he is the Saviour'. The original Greek word for 'Saviour' used here is also used in 1 Timothy 4:10 in which Jesus is described as the 'Saviour of all men'. Therefore, this term does not mean 'the saving blood that justifies God's elect', for not all men are saved. In the context of 1 Timothy 4, this term points more generally to the means by which Christ gives protection and care to all, and this is then applicable in terms of His care and protection to the church in Ephesians 5:23. As a result, it is reinforced in verse 24 that the church submits to Christ and similarly, wives submit to husbands. A husband leads his wife in marriage (more on this in the next section) not because he is superior or better, but because this is his role appointed by God. Therefore, even if the wife is more 'qualified' or 'gifted' to lead and to make decisions, this is not an overriding factor. This is because a wife submits of her own volition in marriage because she has joyfully submitted to and submits to the Lord Jesus Christ. Submission is not conditioned on 'how well he leads' or 'is he loving me as he is commanded?' The motivation, the reason for a wife's submission is Christ! He is the motivation for a wife practically and then joyfully submitting to her husband's leadership for in doing so the Lord gets the Glory!

Nevertheless, a wife's submission does not equate to a passive indifference or silence. A husband and a wife are 'one flesh' and a man's headship and a woman's submission should be built upon an openness in prayer and discussion with one another. As we remind ourselves of Genesis 2, the woman was made from the rib of the man to complement the man, as a companion and a helper to support his leadership because the Lord saw that this was needed! This is why Proverbs 31:10 says, 'An excellent wife who can find? She is far more precious than jewels.'

At the end of verse 24 of Ephesians 5 it says that wives are to submit to their husbands 'in everything'. We should ask if this literally means a wife practically submits in everything? The answer is 'yes' but a qualified 'yes' in light of this passage and using Scripture to answer Scripture. As we have noted, a wife's submission is out of fear of Christ, for every believer's ultimate allegiance is to Him. Therefore, if a husband is not acting Biblically, by leading in a sinful or disobedient way then the wife must say: 'No!' A wife is not called to be a doormat or a pushover. Sometimes, Godly challenge in a loving and submissive way is important in order to complement a husband's headship. As we have noted, a husband is called to be like Christ as head of the church, but any such man is but a fallen sinner who is being graciously restored by the sanctifying work of the Lord Jesus Christ. Therefore, both the husband and wife no longer seek to act independently of each other, but in unity and togetherness as 'one flesh', a wife can submit to her husband whose authority is the Lord Jesus Christ and in whom he trusts and seeks as the 'head' of his wife.

Love

In Ephesians 5:22, the instruction is given to wives that they are to submit to their husbands. It may have been logical to assume that the instruction to men would be to *lead* their wives, and yet that is not what we find in Ephesians 5:25—'Husbands, love your wives ...'

Husbands have a call to love. Wives, submit. Husbands, love. That is interesting, isn't it? It was also quite shocking in this cultural climate of the time of writing. A wife being called to submit to her husband would have been deemed a 'cultural norm' but a husband being called to 'love' his wife certainly wasn't. In our contemporary culture, it may seem absurd to suggest that a husband being called to love his wife is anything other than stating the obvious, but not so. Former Church Minister and theologian William Barclay writes,

> Under Jewish law a woman was a thing, the possession of her husband, just as much as his house or his flocks or his

material goods. She had no legal rights whatever. For instance, under Jewish law, a husband could divorce his wife for any cause, while a wife had no rights whatever in the initiation of divorce; and the only grounds on which a divorce might be awarded her were if her husband developed leprosy, became an apostate or ravished a virgin. In Greek society a respectable woman lived a life of entire seclusion. She never appeared on the streets alone, not even to go marketing. She lived in the women's apartments and did not join her menfolk even for meals. From her there was demanded complete servitude and chastity; but her husband could go out as much as he chose and could enter into as many relationships outside marriage as he liked without incurring any stigma. Under both Jewish and Greek laws and custom all the privileges belong to the husband and all the duties to the wife.[1]

The very fact that a husband is being given instructions for marriage is surprising, but this call to 'love' would have been the ground-breaking teaching in the cultural context. This would have been a penetrating challenge to husbands of that day, but the depth and purpose behind this call for husbands to love their wives is much deeper than this.

This call to love does not diminish a husband's role as head in leading in his marriage but, rather, it explains the root of what it should *look* like. This is evident because of the ongoing comparison given,

> Husbands, love your wives, as Christ loved the church and gave himself up for her, that he might sanctify her, having cleansed her by the washing of water with the word, so that he might present the church to himself in splendour, without spot or wrinkle or any such thing, that she might be holy and without blemish (Ephesians 5:25-27).

Husbands are to 'take their cue' from the Lord Jesus Christ. In Christ, men have the perfect example as head of the church

[1] William Barclay, *The Letters to the Philippians, Colossians, and Thessalonians,* rev. ed. (Philadelphia: Westminster, 1975), 161.

and this headship is grounded in His love for the church. Therefore, we must consider what this word 'love' means.

The word that is used in verse 25 is *agapao*. *Agapao* is the verb of the Greek word *agape,* which is the very nature and heart of who Christ is. This is displayed as *agapao* in the most staggering and glorious way in which He gives of Himself for the sake of His chosen people. This is what is described by the visual picture of the Lord Jesus Christ giving Himself up for the church in verse 25. This then becomes a teaching and a picture of the very heart of Christianity and this is what any husband is to model. Therefore, although this has practical significance to husbands, it is centrally an incredibly relevant teaching to every Christian because it draws our attention to the way by which Jesus Christ loves His church. It also becomes a very profound way by which men can understand what Biblical manhood should look like, namely by looking to Jesus Christ and particularly how He loves and imparts this love. Let's draw out what it is that Christ does for His church in verses 25-27:

- Christ gives Himself for His bride (verse 25) and this is the literal reality in the giving of His life on that cross. The Lord Jesus Christ clothed Himself in human flesh (Philippians 2:7) and came to serve His bride with His life (Mark 10:45).

- Christ loves an *imperfect* bride. Let us be absolutely clear— Christ is not giving Himself up in love because He has a passionate feeling for a beautiful 'friend' of His. Christ's love is one of action for His adulterous, rebellious, sinful bride. Therefore, Christ's love is not based on how great His bride is, it is because of *agapao*.

- Christ *rescues* His bride. The bride of Christ is unclean, unfit for purpose, unworthy of her Saviour and destined for hell. Therefore, Christ does a saving work, giving His very life in order to save her from the pit of hell.

- Christ is *there* for His bride. He doesn't simply do an initial work (glorious and saving though that is!). Ephesians 5:26

writes of Him 'making her holy, cleansing her by the washing of the water of the word'. Christ is doing a work in His people, sanctifying her. This is the reality for the Christian because the Spirit of God is upon us (Acts 2:38), setting us apart, changing and shaping our hearts, deepening our desire for God, our passion and love for His Word, our commitment to pray. Verse 26 is a description of that work which is a work that Christ is doing in His bride.

- Christ makes His bride *beautiful*. In verse 27, we are to be presented radiant, spotless and blameless—and what a picture that is. Christ will make His bride perfect. She will stand beautiful and be 'fit for purpose', made worthy of her bridegroom, the Lord Jesus Christ.

In these brief observations on a mighty section of Scripture we have unravelled a glorious picture. It is a picture that every Christian should meditate upon and delight in and it is this picture of Christ's relationship to His church. We then read in Ephesians 5:28-30,

> In the same way husbands should love their wives as their own bodies. He who loves his wife loves himself. For no one ever hated his own flesh, but nourishes and cherishes it, just as Christ does the church, because we are members of his body.

The unpacking of *agapao* in verses 25-27 is glorious but what a weight of responsibility this is for husbands. Verse 28 then practically applies this to husbands. 'In the same way', husbands are to look to this love of the Lord Jesus Christ to His church and this is how a husband is to love His wife. Incredible!

Below are some of the key components of a husband's 'love' for his wife, which is a very suitable grounding for understanding headship (verse 23) and Biblical manhood:

1. Knowing the Lord

A husband is being given a command here to love modelled upon the Lord Jesus Christ. Therefore, it is fundamental and essential that a husband knows his Lord and Saviour. Everything flows from this in the heart of a believer. Any man seeking to lead his wife according to the Lord's design must stand before the Living God and realise his wretched sinful condition (Isaiah 6:5, Luke 5:8) and yet marvel in awe at the Glorious holiness of God and His merciful loving hand that has been stretched out by the blood of the Lord Jesus Christ. A man who walks in the knowledge that he is a forgiven sinner, living as a disciple of Jesus Christ—this is absolutely crucial and this is particularly crucial for husbands in the context of marriage. Husband, get to know your God and feast upon His Word ... day in, day out. It is why wives are to ask their husbands about Scripture (1 Corinthians 14:35) because God has given husbands this role and He has given the husband this woman, whom He loves far more than this husband ever could, to be His bride. That is a big responsibility and calling and it is why husbands must know the Lord!

2. Thinking as 'one'

The practical instruction of this passage to husbands is absolutely consistent with and consolidates what the Lord says to the man in Genesis 2:24, that the man and woman shall become 'one flesh' (quoted in Ephesians 5:31). A husband therefore must understand clearly that his wife is part of him; they are joined together in the eyes of Almighty God. This is not a matter to be trifled with and not to be belittled, as is often the case in godless relationships. Permit me to share with you the vow that husbands have shared with their wives during marriage ceremonies I have conducted: *I give you this ring as a sign of our marriage. With my body I honour you, all that I am I give to you, and all that I have I share with you within the love of God, Father, Son and Holy Spirit.*

Notice this word 'all'. Husbands are called to treat their wives 'as their own bodies' because they are literally their 'other half'. This mindset and understanding is a crucial base and means by which a husband can and will 'love his wife'. It means that a husband does not think or act independently of his wife, that he should not be 'absent' or 'distant' from her and that he considers everything that he has as being 'everything *we* have'. Therefore, whatever a man would willingly do for his own body, in terms of the care, time and dedication that he gives is time, care and dedication given to the 'collective we', namely his wife as well as himself by literally treating his wife as though she was his body for they are 'one' in the eyes of the Lord. This is a very crucial point that will be unravelled in greater practical and spiritual depth in later chapters.

3. Leading sacrificially

A reminder of verses 25-27 is the ideal framework for understanding the Lord Jesus Christ as one who leads *sacrificially*. Jesus takes the lead with decisive action by the fact that He came to rescue and to perfect His bride, the church. This is the pinnacle of leadership and of Biblical manhood! We can clearly then infer that any notion of a husband's leadership being that of 'I'm in charge and the wife must serve me and my needs' is a redundant and repugnant concept. The Lord Jesus was strong in leadership in His decision-making and actions, but these were the actions of One who came sacrificially in order to serve His bride. We see this evidenced by His actions (washing the disciples' feet, laying down His life on the cross) and by His teaching about how we can be great by being last and servant of all (Mark 9:35). Husbands are to follow this model of leadership which is not so much a right but a weight of responsibility ordained by the Living God!

A husband who practically, emotionally, spiritually leads in such a way points to Jesus Christ in his marriage and what a joy for any wife to submit to such a head in marriage. A servant leader is therefore one who submits to the Lord Jesus Christ (Ephesians 5:21) and seeks to lead in a way where he can point his wife to her Saviour, the perfect bridegroom. A servant leader is one who is willing to sacrifice for the sake of his wife. A servant leader is ready to serve his wife for the sake of her spiritual well-being and the health of their marriage. A servant leader will make decisions not for his own end, but out of fear for the Lord and love for his wife (consider the first two points above). This is why the call to husbands is to 'love' because it is love that underpins a husband's leadership as the head of his wife.

4. Providing for her needs

There is therefore a practical outworking of a man's leadership in love. He has a responsibility as the head of his wife to provide for her.

The Lord Jesus literally put His body on the line by dying for His wife. Husbands should be willing and ready to do likewise. As the head of the family, in love, treating his wife as his own body, there is a readiness to throw your entire body on the line, even sacrifice your very life, in order to protect your wife. This is a husband's role in marriage and it requires bravery and strength in the Lord!

It can also be inferred from this passage and others (1 Timothy 5:8) that a husband is to provide for the physical needs of his wife and family. In Genesis, the man is given the role of working in the garden and it is therefore his responsibility to ensure that the family is financially stable and supported. There may be circumstances in which a man may be unable to work and there is not a Biblical command against a woman working in paid employment, but the commands for the provision of the family are given to men and the responsibility within the home and for children are given to women (Titus 2:3-5).

The Lord Jesus also provides mightily for the spiritual well-being of His bride and husbands are to do likewise. Therefore husbands have a spiritual responsibility for the well-being of their wives which involves:

- Leading family devotions, being able to teach the Scriptures and lead in prayer.
- Speaking with their wives, asking about their spiritual walk, providing encouragement and timely loving rebuke.
- Protecting her from spiritual danger by taking the lead in fighting any sinful influence or deceptive/destructive path.

The call to 'love' for a husband complements a wife's call to submission for this word more effectively elaborates what a husband's headship looks like in practice. An abusive tyrant or the man of lazy indifference spending more time 'in front of the box with a can' than leading his family is in no way the head of his wife in accordance with Scripture and this is why understanding the Biblical framework given in this passage is crucial. It is also why any marriage should be a celebration and a metaphor of the majestic and perfect love of the Lord Jesus Christ for His church. What a testimony and what a Gospel witness marriage is when understood and applied according to Scripture.

Profound Mystery

There is one final component of this passage that underpins much of what has been considered in this Chapter, namely, the 'mystery' of marriage. Ephesians 5:31-33,

> 'Therefore a man shall leave his father and mother and hold fast to his wife, and the two shall become one flesh.' This mystery is profound, and I am saying that it refers to Christ and the church. However, let each one of you love his wife as himself, and let the wife see that she respects her husband.

It is very deliberate and profound that Genesis 2:24 is quoted in verse 31. The Apostle Paul then describes this mystery as 'profound' referring to Christ and the church, and it may seem like a mystery as to what this is all about!

In Genesis 2:24 we have the institution of marriage given by God to the male and female who have been created perfect in His image. This is a beautiful thing, and it is without flaw. However, mankind fell away in sin, disobeying God and ultimately being condemned. So what of human relationships? What of the institution of marriage? It is here where this mystery becomes so profound. In 1 Corinthians 15 there is a distinct comparison given between the first man, Adam, and the second man, Jesus Christ (1 Corinthians 15:47). 1 Corinthians 15:20-22,

> But in fact Christ has been raised from the dead, the firstfruits of those who have fallen asleep. For as by a man came death, by a man has come also the resurrection of the dead. For as in Adam all die, so also in Christ shall all be made alive.

In these verses, there is the clear consequence of the first man's fall, namely death. However, this is contrasted with the Lord Jesus Christ, for in Him there comes life, life everlasting. This contrast becomes very applicable now in relation to the mystery of marriage. Back in the Garden of Eden, the man was perfect but incomplete, and therefore the woman was made from the man and made to be a companion for the man. This was the design of the Lord in marriage, which was then destroyed by sin entering the world, resulting in death. Therefore, the attention then moves to the 'second man', from heaven, Jesus Christ. His bride, the church also comes *from* Him, by the saving work on the cross for His blood is what saves and is the means by which the church is formed and grows. Thus, the institution of marriage is now grounded in the restoration of God's people, through Christ and His saving and perfecting His bride. This is a profound mystery and a glorious one at that!

There is even greater depth to this mystery. There are mighty passages of Scripture such as John 1:1-14 and Colossians 1:15-20 that give in-depth teaching of the perfect unity of Father, Son and Spirit and that the Son, Jesus Christ, is fully God and He is Glorious. However, we see that Christ becomes a man, fully man (John 1:14, Philippians 2:6-7) whilst being fully divine, to join together with His bride, the church. This is His reason for coming. Therefore, it would take His very death on the cross, where the Father forsook the Son (Matthew 27:45-46) because He was taking the penalty for the sins of His bride in order to rescue and perfect her. This is the profound mystery of Christ and the church (Ephesians 5:32) and what a glorious mystery this is! The mystery of Christ and the church not only becomes the metaphor for every earthly marriage, an institution given before the Fall, thus providing a glorious safeguard in the face of sin, but it also is the means by which the church is adopted into

Christ's family (Ephesians 1:5) and blessed with eternal life with our God. This is a teaching that every Christian must know of and give all the Glory to the Living God.

As we work through many practical questions and considerations within marriages today, we must remind ourselves that every marriage consists of two fallen sinners who are restored by grace and in desperate need of grace. This is why husbands and wives must 'get to grips' with the Scriptures and feast their eyes on the rich delights of the Word of God. Therefore, in answer to the question posed at the beginning of this Chapter, Biblical marriage is absolutely essential. A marriage that is not understood as being instituted by God, where men and women have been made to complement each other in relationship together and where Christ's relationship with the church becomes the metaphor of every marriage relationship thus becomes something very different (and unbiblical) indeed. However, with this framework in place, we can therefore consider and apply Scripture at the heart of what is discussed in the consequent Chapters for the sake of Glorifying God and for the health and growth of any marriage.

2

EXPECTATION

IT WAS ONLY a few years ago that Binglin and I were dating and I can still vividly remember the feelings. I thought about her many times throughout the day. I would even go onto her Facebook page and look at some of her pictures and smile at how beautiful she was and how much I loved her. I would spend much time thinking about my messages that I sent to her. I would make considerable effort with how I dressed. I would plan our times together carefully. I would ensure that I was romantic, spontaneously giving her flowers or arranging a surprise trip somewhere. We were motivated to spend time with each other, sacrificing other 'otherwise priorities' and so it soon became that we were daily spending time with each other. I even took odd occasions to (attempt to) cook for her despite my incompetence in this area!

This sounds nice, doesn't it? I look back, and I smile. And some of you may question why I am *looking back?* In fact, some may even go as far as to think (and say!) in response, *'Well, my relationship will always be passionate. We are in love.'* Now it isn't my intention to throw a wet blanket over anyone's enthusiasm! But it is important that the topic of *expectation* is carefully considered, as this is an area that can so often lead to or has been the cause of many struggles and a potential breakdown in a marriage.

Unrealistic expectations

The early stages of a relationship are often filled with 'passion' and 'romance' but sometimes these can become the breeding ground for unrealistic expectations. If you consider a potentially typical example from my own experience you will quickly realise how *intense* that time was. During this period, how much time is spent thinking about that person, how much effort is put into your appearance, how much you are willing to sacrifice for that person and ask, is that sustainable in the long run? The reality is that many people enter into relationships as though they were entering a sprint as opposed to a long-distance run. If you began a long-distance run as though you were running a sprint then what is going to happen? You will be in the lead, it will all be very impressive and then you will inevitably and very quickly run out of steam and soon crash and burn.

And yet, the romantic novel or film of the 'young girl's dream' will consistently paint a picture of a whirlwind romance and then a 'happily ever after' relationship involving the dashing knight (or prince) who is strong and brave, and the sweet, defenceless girl (princess, really) who is swept off her feet. This 'lifetime of happiness/happily ever after' picture is the brief conclusion to the story, but what does this consist of? What would the expectation, the hope, the dream be? Perhaps the husband and wife live in a nice home, with lovely kids, and to add the *Christian part,* are actively serving in their local church. Now, the practical outworkings of this 'dream marriage' may become reality in places, and yet it can so easily and so often become the 'carrot that Satan dangles' in front of a young couple that can be utterly destructive. Perhaps this illustration can help; imagine moving into a house and you dream of having a beautiful garden. That sounds nice until you realise the work and effort involved to remove dead plants, get rid of the hundreds of weeds, start growing new plants, pruning what is already there

... what a lot of hassle! In order to enjoy the blessing of marriage, of which there is great blessing, it involves a lot of hard work and realism.

The problem is that we often paint an unrealistic picture of ourselves as well as having unrealistic expectations of our spouse! This will often then lead to many a husband or a wife later asking, what has changed? The man may wonder why his wife has become such a 'nag', always complaining, always undermining his authority? *She was so sweet and encouraging before!* The woman will wonder why he has become so lazy and disinterested, why he doesn't notice how she dresses or give her any spontaneous gifts anymore? *He has changed!*

But realistically, what often changes is that the relationship 'progresses' from performance to realism. It became very clear to me early into my marriage that *who you really are* is exposed to your spouse. The day in, day out reality of marriage is certainly an immense blessing (as we will explore through these Chapters) but it is also a sobering reality. The day-to-day reality is not perfect hair, beautiful make up and attractive clothing. The reality *can often be* dishevelled hair, a spotty face, comfortable clothing accompanied by bad breath, undesirable bodily noises and lingering smells in the toilet! The day-to-day reality is not the undivided attention of your spouse and a willingness to 'drop everything' to please you.

Therefore, the prevalent question is not 'what changed' but rather, 'what has been exposed'? For example, when Binglin and I were dating, I sometimes chose to spend time with her instead of watching a big football match that I wanted to see. However, after we got married, I chose the big football match and *kindly invited* her to watch the game with me. So what has changed? Nothing has changed but something has been exposed. My selfishness. In both instances, I have chosen what makes *me* most happy. In the first instance, Binglin and I are in the early stages of a relationship and so it is in my best interests to make a special effort to build the relationship and also it is very new and exciting. In the second instance, Binglin and I are married.

We're a 'done deal'. I don't *need* to make the right impression. We are a lot more comfortable with each other.

As fallen sinners, the desire of our heart is ourselves and the glory of self. Therefore, this is what directs us in what we do. This often means high intensity effort early into a relationship because it is in our interests to build up the relationship as well as the human instinct to put special effort into something new, fresh and exciting. This often then means that this intensity wanes on our part as the relationship progresses, but the expectations we have of our spouse will remain very high! At every stage, we can so 'naturally' do things, sometimes that are outwardly kind or selfless with a heart that is motivated and driven for the sake of serving self! This is therefore the danger that must be dissected in order to understand how we can have Biblically driven expectations that can produce a marriage that is even greater than the 'whirlwind romance and happily ever after *Hollywood* dream'.

Exposing the self-serving heart

It is startling to note that an increasing false teaching has corrupted many churches, which goes along the lines of, 'God loves you just the way you are and wants to bless you.' If we apply this theology to the topic of marriage then we are in big trouble! This theology infers that you are not perfect but that doesn't matter because we worship a loving God who loves you. This man-centred theology not only creates a lopsided theology of the attributes of God, but it also drastically sets sinful man up for a big, big fall!

We can identify clearly in Scripture that man's great danger is that he has placed self in the place of the Living God. You are the main player. This theology inadvertently supports this sinful premise because it effectively says, 'Yes, you are a *sinner* but God loves you ... God wants big things for you.' God becomes the supporting cast in your 'you-centred' world where God is working to bless and care for you. This is not only unbiblical and irreverent, but it also feeds the sinful, self-serving desires of self that can crush relationships. It is thus crucial to have a right theology of the saving work of Christ and His sanctifying work in our lives. And so we should alternatively read, 'God loves you too much to keep you the way that you are, and the cross is the visible picture of how serious your sin actually is as well as how great His love is.'

If then, as Christians, you enter into marriage with expectations about how this marriage and your spouse can and will fulfil *your* needs then there are two major problems here. First, you are placing your hope in a fellow sinner who will let you down! Second, you are failing to place your hope, practically, in the One in whom you have the very gift of eternal life—Jesus Christ.

You may stop here and think to yourself, 'Yes, I get it. Our hope must be in Christ. But my marriage is a mess! I didn't think I expected too much of my husband but he is impossible.'

Many marriages that reach a point where they have 'broken down' will be the 'grounds for divorce' in the eyes of the world. And yet, because of Christ, this could be an act of grace! Let's consider the lesson learned by the prodigal son in this parable in Luke 15:11-16,

> And he said, "There was a man who had two sons. And the younger of them said to his father, 'Father, give me the share of property that is coming to me.' And he divided his property between them. Not many days later, the younger son gathered all he had and took a journey into a far country, and there he squandered his property in reckless living. And when he had spent everything, a severe famine arose in that country, and he began to be in need. So he went and hired himself out to one of the citizens of that country, who sent him into his fields to feed pigs. And he was longing to be fed with the pods that the pigs ate, and no one gave him anything.

At the beginning of this parable, the younger son 'has it all' and by verse 16 he has 'nothing'. It may shock you to realise that the son is in a better place in verse 16 than he is at the beginning of this parable. Does that make sense? At face value, no. Practically speaking, it is obviously better to be with your loving family, have great wealth, a home, food to eat than to have nothing. Yet what has taken place in this man's heart is pivotal. Initially, he is motivated by a desire to serve himself to the extent where he demands his father's inheritance, inferring that he wishes him dead! He believes that he can serve himself best by getting all of this stuff *now* and he expects that this will satisfy him and bring him happiness. But it does not. As he squanders his inheritance, it simply exposes a heart that desired self-glory which can only lead to dissatisfaction and despair. By the time the younger son is sitting with the pigs, broken and penniless, this despair that he faces on all levels becomes an act of grace. Why? Because God has brought him to a point in his life where his self-serving desires have been exposed in a brutal and painful fashion, which leads to a genuine conviction of sin. What follows is a beautiful story of redemption where this son abandons the desire to serve himself and goes to his father with a heart of repentance and a willingness to serve.

In marriage, it can take the realisation that your spouse is 'not the person you married' or even the 'breakdown' in marriage for the Lord to convict *your* heart. If your spouse has been the source of 'meeting your expectations' then it is the grace of God that this expectation is shattered, at whatever stage in a relationship/marriage. Man's need is not met in finding ways and means of serving self but by coming to Christ as convicted sinners and realising that our need is only met by who Christ is and what He has done. When we come to Christ in repentance and faith, like the prodigal son, we come as exposed and unworthy sinners with a Spirit-driven willingness and a desire now to serve the One who has graciously rescued us! Life for the Christian now becomes about Jesus Christ and the advance of His Kingdom and the Glory of His Name.

What impact does this have for any given married couple? It has a glorious, Christ-exalting impact. Instead of two sinners who expect their spouse to fulfil their selfish needs, you have two forgiven sinners who come to Christ who has fulfilled their greatest need and come with an expectation to serve sacrificially as opposed to being served.

Realistic expectations

On the first occasion that Binglin and I went out together for a coffee ourselves it was certainly a memorable and exciting 3-hour epic! One interesting reflection that Binglin had after this time was how many negative things that I said about myself. In truth, I had thought myself to be quite a confident person. However, she said that she was surprised as to how open I was about my weaknesses particularly as we didn't know each other very well. This would not normally be the method of 'impressing a girl'. In response I quipped that it was good for her impression of me to start off low because then things can only improve as we go on!

Why have I mentioned this? This is not the practical suggestion that we ought to verbally batter ourselves to avoid giving a false impression. But we must ask ourselves, from the very beginning, what impression do we want to make to our future spouse? We want to make a good impression, right? Similarly with our church, at our work, we want to make a good impression. We want to cover up weaknesses, mistakes, *sin*. In response to this, let me make it clear that one of the biggest points that has a bearing on the consequent Chapters is understanding clearly *who* we are as Christians. We did not come to God seeking to make a good impression. We also didn't need to make a bad impression, but simply, we come to God exposed as the rebellious sinners that we are. Therefore, there are Chapters on issues such as blame, trust, lust because this is our battleground as sinners who have been forgiven by grace. This is what we must realistically expect in marriage.

My wife told me about a conversation between two of her unmarried friends in which they concluded that even on their wedding day they couldn't be 100% sure that the person they were about to marry would be the one they should spend their life with. They went on to ask, how can you be sure? In response to this, I reflected on how such thinking was symptomatic of unrealistic expectations in marriage. When a person is about to get married, if they know enough about their spouse then there is undoubtedly a long list of reasons to make them unsure and certainly not 100%. That's not comforting, is it? Well it depends what your expectations are. When Binglin retold this conversation between her friends I proceeded to ask her what can make her 100% that we are right to be married. The answer? We are married. God has instituted marriage, He has knit us together as one flesh which is binding for all of our lives. Of course, we are not compatible in some ways and, of course, we have flaws that don't meet the criteria of our 'dream spouse'—and this is the point of this Chapter. However, we can be sure that marriage is of the Lord and is a rich blessing for those whose needs are met *savingly* and eternally in Jesus Christ.

Sacrificial foundations

I think it is also important to dispel the notion that the initial romance in a marriage is therefore a bad thing. It is a good, exciting and truly special thing. However, relationships naturally mature and so should the romance. In my life, I have enjoyed many new and exciting things but the things that I cherish most are those that have become valuable to me. A number of weeks after my son was born our house was burgled and a number of items were taken. The greatest sadness was not the loss of my car, money or electronic devices, but my watch. This was my grandfather's watch, which I was given when I was 15 years old after he died. This watch was old, I was used to it and comfortable with it, but with time, it became more precious. It is my prayer that this is the testimony of the growing Christian in their relationship with Jesus Christ and consequently in relation to their spouse. It is very easy to buy flowers and chocolates weeks into a relationship, but how precious it is to do a similar act years into a marriage. This is not a gimmick. This is not a game to try to impress. This is rooted in a love that is deep towards one that you cherish more and more. It is why I am genuinely overjoyed to see a married couple of many decades walking hand in hand, speaking affectionately towards each other. The Christian can genuinely expect this in marriage, because Christ brings about the change and gives the direction in how we are to live.

The Word of God gives a clear picture of the mystery of marriage being a metaphor of Christ's relationship to His bride, the church. In this picture, we have the bridegroom acting in love sacrificially for His bride for the Glory of God. This sort of relationship does not come naturally to fallen sinners and yet for two forgiven sinners this is the picture of such a marriage because it is a marriage built on grace. Grace turns the hearts of two self-serving sinners into disciples of the One who came to serve, sacrificially. This is the basis for the practical instructions to husbands and wives in Ephesians 5 and why our expectation can be one of deep love, joy, romance and passion in the face of the every day battles of married life. You may be fighting with a sinner in marriage, you are certainly fighting against your sinful self, but you stand together united in the victory of Jesus Christ. He is the reason that we can dismiss unrealistic expectations that merely set us up for relational breakdowns and yet still have hope and the basis for an even greater expectation. Because our hope, our joy, our desire, our need is met in Christ and we can expect the blessing of a marriage that is grounded in this saving reality between two unworthy sinners who have been forgiven and are being sanctified by His wondrous, sweet and precious grace.

3

BLAME

Know this, my beloved brothers: let every person be quick to hear, slow to speak, slow to anger.—James 1:19

Why do you see the speck that is in your brother's eye, but do not notice the log that is in your own eye?—Matthew 7:3

ONE OF THE most common issues that arises in any human relationship, particularly between a married couple, is the earnest and natural desire to elevate self and chastise your spouse as the one who has wronged you, whilst being oblivious to any wrong-doing on your own part. This is the natural instinct of children in the playground and adults are often not much better!

Teacher: What happened?
Child: He said nasty words to me.
Teacher: And did you do anything to cause this or to upset him?
Child: No.

Permit me to elaborate this point with a typical example from my marriage: On my day off, I had made plans to take Binglin to a scenic spot and then perhaps go to a nice café to do a Bible study together. Everything was planned, although I hadn't discussed this with her. Binglin later announces that she needs to go to a couple of shops to return some items and that we could do this on our day off ... and perhaps we can look at some more shops! I agree to this. However, inwardly I am not happy but think to myself, 'I'm a good husband. I'm relinquishing my plans in order to make her happy.'

On the day itself, I have mentally adjusted (or so I think) to the rough plan for the day and, initially, things are fine and my wife seems happy. However, as we go from shop to shop, my initial enthusiasm has waned and Binglin doesn't even seem that happy as she can't find the dress she wants to buy! In addition, my lack of interest in the matter is adding to the tension. Therefore, I am becoming increasingly irritable and impatient because after all *I am the one who is doing this for her!* Inevitably, tensions run high, both Binglin and I start to become angry, we begin to argue and we head back to the car for a period of sulking and silence.

Later, Binglin then speaks to me, visibly upset and asking why I haven't been speaking to her and taking the initiative to sort the problem. I respond initially in a manner that justifies my actions as well as seeking to accuse Binglin as the guilty party, but by now, time has given me perspective, an opportunity to calm down and reflect, and I begin to make steps towards reconciliation.

The problems

This is a typical example from the early days of our marriage but this is not entirely confined to history. My wife and I are battling in a spiritual war against our sinful desires and tendencies and it is only by the grace of God sanctifying our hearts and our marriage that we can press on to maturity. Let's now draw out two problems in this very 'typical' example.

1. We had different plans

One of the absolute certainties in any marriage is that on many, many occasions, you will have one plan and your spouse will have a different plan. As a result, given the nature of becoming 'one flesh' and what we saw that looked like in Chapter 1, we have a problem!

Let me identify the positive point in this example, which is that I have not thought and planned independently of my wife. It is absolutely crucial to understand the need to dedicate time *for* your spouse, and I believe this is primarily important for husbands as leaders in decision making.

Let's now consider the reality. Initially, I had planned our day, but a decision had not been made. Is there a valid argument to suggest, 'You're the husband, you've made the plan, the wife should submit!'? Simply put, no. A husband's leadership and decision-making must incorporate two vital components here. First, the desire to put Christ at the centre, and, second, the needs of his wife above his own. Therefore, it is important to realise that as a husband I will be prone to make plans and seek to make decisions with selfish intentions at heart. Also, even if my plans are purely selfless and for the sake of Christ and then my wife, communication with her is still important before a decision is made, particularly if the decisions directly and practically concern her. (There are going to be times where decisions are made without communication due to it being a surprise, or because it is a small 'every day' matter, or because it was already agreed that one of you will make decisions on a particular area/issue in your day-to-day marriage.)

In this example, like many others, I have made plans and Binglin has had other plans. So, what next? Was it right for me to relinquish my plans in order to make her happy? Is this the Biblical model of marriage? It seems like a fairly selfless, good deed?

Well, let's give thanks to the Lord Jesus Christ that He did not simply look to the external, but He looked to the heart throughout the Gospels. Although I have done a seemingly good thing, my wife and I have already both made mistakes here.

First, my wife has stated her desire for the day without considering or asking what I had maybe planned or wanted to do. Her plan for the day was not a sinful thing, but to understand the practical outworking of living as 'one flesh' requires ongoing and often, constant consideration of each other's feelings and desires.

Second, on my part, there has been a distinct lack of communication at a crucial time, which proves to be a catalyst for the ensuing problem. It is good that a man makes plans, particularly plans involving a husband and wife spending time together, and doubly so to spend time studying the Word of God. These are good plans. However, as soon as Binglin has stated her desire to do something on that day, there is a problem that needs to be addressed. She has not set out to upset me; her plans are a perfectly normal and a recreational thing for a couple to do. However, this has not pleased me. Why? Because I am being selfish. She has disrupted *my* plans! This is the root of the problem and this is where the understanding of 'love' in a marriage must be unpacked. Do I love my wife as Christ loves the church? In practice, this is in question in a situation here. My sinful disposition is that I love *me* and I love me being 'so loving towards my wife by planning such a special day'. As soon as that is ruined, my real love in this situation, namely myself, is wounded. My desire for my plans, my ways, have been attacked, and now I face the growing sense of frustration and resentment and the consequent desire to target the 'guilty party'.

So what should happen here? If I am overcome by my selfishness and if it harbours negative feelings in my heart, then I must repent before the Lord and should communicate this with my wife. At times when the situation may be more serious, it may be wise to take time to pray and seek counsel from the Lord, but pretence will achieve nothing here. I am not being 'selfless' by ignoring my displeasure and resentment—instead, I am still being selfish. Only now, I am being more infantile! As I have already stated, I am making a mental note of my 'outward good deed' during this day, which is simply loading the metaphorical gun that I plan to fire at the opportune time. In a situation where we feel hurt, upset or frustrated, this ought to be communicated.

It is important to stress, there is a right and a wrong way to communicate. In this example, I might say to Binglin, 'I planned to take you somewhere scenic and then do a Bible study. That's far more important than going shopping! I'm not happy about this.'

It is good that I have made my feelings clear, but I have done this in an inappropriate manner. Is not the desire of a Christ-exalting husband or wife to *resolve* any inner/outward conflict? If we seek to communicate our feelings then we must be motivated to fight for a positive solution. Otherwise, this form of communication simply becomes the platform for accusation and blame, again submitting to the selfish desires of the heart.

Alternatively, I could say to Binglin, 'I planned to take you somewhere scenic and then do a Bible study. And because you've said you wanted to do something different, I feel angry about this. And this is sinful, because I wanted things my own way. Can we pray together?'

This may seem 'over the top' over a trivial matter such as what a couple does with a day off, but it can often be the smaller situations that build up and can set very bad and damaging patterns in a marriage relationship. Because, let's be clear, the heart issues are big and they need to be addressed no matter how big or small the situation or circumstance may be. This is such an important consideration for any couple in fighting for their marriage. We are coming together as two sinners, with different objectives and agendas, and we must fight in our marriages to seek Christ and to be like Him!

2. We played the 'blame game'

It goes without saying that had the aforementioned principles been applied then the practical outworking of the day itself ought to have been radically different regardless of what we ended up doing. Nevertheless, we may often still find ourselves in situations or doing things that we don't want to be doing which can easily lead to conflict, as this one most certainly did. Now, after Binglin and I have both become increasingly frustrated and expressed that in no uncertain terms to each other, thus leading to an argument, how must this be resolved?

Let's firstly consider the merits of a period of silence after an argument. In this example, Binglin and I have reached a stage where we are angry at each other, which leads to a period of silence. It is obvious that silence leads to no resolution but many will argue that it is an important time for the people involved to calm down, maybe even to pray, and get some much needed perspective. This, at times, would be a wise thing to do. However, not in the way that we did it, and many others often do! If you have had an argument and then stop speaking to each other, this merely becomes the platform for an open wound to fester and rot. In my experience, a time of silence after an argument has been a cause of great distress to my wife because this is a time when I do not communicate my love, care and protection for my wife. This is a time where I sentence her to the silence of my anger until further notice. Instead, it becomes very important even at the time of great anger or upset to even simply state, 'I need some time. Let's talk later. I love you.'

We are fighting against a formidable enemy in Satan, and he has many tools at his disposal. During the times of rage and frustration, he will happily massage the ego of your pride, he will happily support your arguments for self-justification, he will wilfully make you 'get on with things' instead of sorting the problem, thus allowing the 'wound' to fester. Yes, Satan takes those nice, big, dark sins and sugar coats them in all sorts of attractive colours and flavours. In my time of upset and in the silence, I can so easily submit to the sinful desires of my heart and not seek resolution, because after all, *she doesn't deserve it after the way she has treated me.* Now, this principle applies to both a husband and a wife. It is important to emphasise a husband's role in taking the initiative to sort an issue of contention or conflict. However, both husband and wife must be ready to battle the urge to 'play the blame game'.

Lesson from the Garden of Eden
In Chapter 1 (of this book) we studied the designed order of creation and the relationship between the man and woman in Genesis

2. The following Chapter contains the infamous Fall of man when the serpent tempts the woman to eat from the tree that God explicitly told them not to eat from. The woman disobeys God, as does the man. They fall in their sin, thus smashing the beautiful perfect relationship that man has with Almighty God. It is at the point when the man and woman have eaten that we read this interesting account in Genesis 3:9-13,

> But the Lord God called to the man and said to him, 'Where are you?' And he said, 'I heard the sound of you in the garden, and I was afraid, because I was naked, and I hid myself.' He said, 'Who told you that you were naked? Have you eaten of the tree of which I commanded you not to eat?' The man said, 'The woman whom you gave to be with me, she gave me fruit of the tree, and I ate.' Then the Lord God said to the woman, 'What is this that you have done?' The woman said, 'The serpent deceived me, and I ate.'

It is certainly noteworthy to see *whom* the Lord addresses in response to the sinful actions of the man and the woman, thus emphasising a man's responsibility as the servant leader of the family! However, notice the response of the man. When asked what he has done, what does he do? He replies with, 'The woman …' As soon as we read these words, we understand what's happening here. The man is abdicating his responsibility as a man and he is also not taking responsibility for his own actions. This is the blame game! And what of the woman? Because, as we see earlier in Genesis 3, she is the instigator after the serpent effectively targets the disruption of God's designed roles for men and women! How does the woman respond when the Lord confronts her? Again, verse 13, 'The serpent …' Same thing, the blame game.

As sin enters the world, a frighteningly realistic and common pattern has emerged in response to sin … 'He did it', 'it's her fault'. What's going on here? In the Garden of Eden, in the example from my marriage, and in countless other situations? It's the natural reaction of the sinner's heart. When I am confronted with a situation that has resulted or may result in conflict, I have two metaphorical implements to help indulge and support *sinful me.* First, my rose-tinted glasses. My rose-tinted glasses are helpful when I look in the mirror and simply consider me, and my actions in a situation. They make me and my actions look much more rosy than they are. Therefore, I will naturally elevate myself, my actions, as being right. Second, my microscope. I need my microscope to closely examine and dissect the flaws of the other person. This is helpful because this gives me a much stronger opportunity to accuse and blame the person for all their wrong-doing, and maybe much more. I also find the microscope helps me to wear my rose-tinted glasses with greater assurance. Now, this almost comical picture can highlight a simple and yet profound point in any sinner's heart. It is so natural to elevate self and condemn others because this is what man has done in his heart before the Living God! From that point in the Garden of Eden, man has actively sought to dethrone God of His Right and Glorious place in their hearts. That place now *belongs* to the self. This is the sinner's disposition and it sadly becomes natural that one's actions will follow based on this disposition, namely, the desire for our own glory.

It is crucial then that we remind ourselves of what it *looks like in practice* to live our lives as disciples of the Lord Jesus Christ. We are not simply 'Christian' by name, but by the regeneration of our being, we are born again (John 3:3) in Jesus Christ. This means that we have been set free from sin which leads to death (Romans 6:22-23) and we no longer desire the things of the flesh but the Spirit (Romans 8:5-9). Therefore, the Spirit of the Living God is doing a mighty work of sanctifying the born again believer and this will be, at times, a painful and an unpleasant process. There is a lot of 'dross' and 'debris' in the heart and life of a sinner and Christ is shining a big, bright light upon this. Thus, when we do wrong, when we sin, our Lord through His Word will expose that. This is what He does in the heart of any unforgiven sinner who comes to Christ in saving faith and this is the work He is doing in our lives as His followers. Therefore, what a battle that is when we realise how easy, comfortable and natural it has been/is to fall back on the default position of 'self-glorification', where the rose-tinted glasses for self and the microscope for others is prevalent. In Christ, we *must* wage war with this! In Christ, in our marriages, we *must* wage war with the desire to play the 'blame game'. The reality is that when two sinners have conflict there are two sinners who must prayerfully reflect and examine their own hearts, address their own problems, and at times, remove their own 'plank' before trying to remove the other's 'speck' from their eye (Matthew 7:3-5).

So how do we take on this fight?
In the example from my marriage, the natural desire in my heart, and Binglin's heart, was to blame the other person for wrong doing. In a similar fashion, this is what we see the man and woman doing in the Garden of Eden before God: the man blames the woman, the woman blames the serpent. Therefore, we must STOP before we sharpen the blade ready to attack. It is likely that this crucial step will, in many cases, already lead to enough of a God-given realisation of the sinful ways by which we have acted. However, what if you still believe you are the innocent party? In almost all of these situations, it is highly likely you need more time to prayerfully examine your heart. But let's imagine that in this dispute with my wife, I was completely innocent and she was the instigator of all wrongdoing. Am I then justified in my silence, waiting for her to come to me and apologise? No! If a husband and a wife get to a stage where they are arguing, and it causes upset on both parties, then there is already something to sort out! Even during an instance where you are the innocent party, or perhaps, the 'less guilty' party, if you have caused upset then that is in itself enough of a reason to examine your heart and then to apologise.

I remember, when I was 20 years old, getting into an argument with a female friend, and we were both arguing our case and she then stopped me completely in my tracks. Why? She said, 'I'm sorry I've upset you.' Was she the instigator of the problem or was I? It doesn't matter. She saw that we had got to a situation where conflict had arisen and that was enough of a motivator for her to apologise. This is a practical example of a very potent verse in Proverbs 28:13, 'Whoever conceals his transgressions will not prosper, but he who confesses and forsakes them will obtain mercy.'

How quick we are to speak and to accuse and yet how slow we are to stop, pray, listen and apologise. However, this need not be the ongoing disposition of your sinful heart in marriage. This is because we can now truly rest in the knowledge that the 'peace of Christ rules in our hearts' (Colossians 3:15) and the cross of Jesus Christ is the victory cry and living hope by which we cling for dear life and a life of sanctification by the Spirit of the Living God. I am thankful to the Lord that based on the teaching of His Word and the sanctifying work of the Holy Spirit in our hearts that my wife and I are gradually learning to practically apply the desire we have to live like Christ in the 'every day' situations of marriage. The desire to blame your spouse is a classic disposition of a man or woman who is prone to think and act based on their own glory. This is no more than pride, and it is why we daily must cleave to Christ and praise God for His grace at work in our lives. It can only be by the grace of God that you will seek to speak openly when you are upset with a desire to reconcile rather than accuse. It is only by grace that you will respond to hurt and upset caused by conflict in a manner that is befitting of Jesus Christ.

You cannot do this in and of yourself, but only because you now live in Christ, with Christ and for Christ. The impact that Christ has upon our lives is not confined to the archives of a 'one off' decision securing something nice when we die. The Lord Jesus Christ came to die for sinners to the Glory of His Name and this changes everything in the life of the Christian because our hearts now belong to Him. It means that our life is not lived for ourselves, but for Christ, and that God's Glory is the chief end, not our own. To meditate upon this truth will have a radical impact on any marriage because it transforms our worldview and shapes our realisation that we are fighting against the carnal nature and what is the sinful disposition. Therefore, in times of anger and frustration particularly with our spouse, it is the reality of the Gospel and its impact in your life that is transformative. It is why my prayer is that in my marriage and in countless marriages, we will approach the times of conflict with a prayerful longing to look 'through the lens of the cross' with a willingness to examine our own hearts first, be ready to apologise for hurt and wrong-doing, and be willing to speak openly with a view to reconcile, not to accuse.

4

TRUST

But Jesus on his part did not entrust himself to them, because he knew all people and needed no one to bear witness about man, for he himself knew what was in man.—John 2:24-25

THE DAY AFTER Binglin and I got married, we headed straight to the 'surprise destination' for our honeymoon. After we had arrived and settled into our accommodation I said to Binglin how much I loved her and would do everything I could to protect her and care for her. However, I was very clear that I am a weak and sinful man and on many levels am not the husband that she, as the woman I love, deserves. Is this a self-pitying attempt at being self-effacing in order for my wife to reaffirm how incredible I am and how 'lucky' she is? Absolutely not.

Why you cannot trust your spouse
During the early stages of our marriage, I also spoke to Binglin about the issue of 'trust' in our marriage and I stated quite clearly that in and of myself, she cannot *trust* me. Is this controversial?

Is it unbiblical? If she can't trust me, then why should she be married to me?

The Hebrew word for 'trust' in Scripture is *batach* which means to be 'careless', namely, being without a care or concern due to the feeling, the safety, you have with this person. Therefore, when a wife is commanded by Scripture to 'submit to her husband in everything' (Ephesians 5:24), is there not surely a necessity for trust in a way that is almost without concern for the safety and security that you have with your husband? Absolutely!

However, have I not already stressed to my wife that she *cannot* trust me? Yes, I have.

This does not then become an attempt by me to sound 'clever', but rather, the means by which a genuine, unbreakable trust is understood and established in a marriage. This will not be achieved in a marriage by saying, 'My spouse is perfect and he/she would never let me down.' The problem with such thinking, romantic and positive though it may be, is that it is simply not true. As a husband, I examine my heart and see that there are many ways I have and am capable of letting Binglin down. I see the dangers I face in this spiritual war in a sinful world, and so the base for genuine 'without care' trust in marriage must be rooted and found in the arms of King Jesus!

Trust in the Lord

In Psalm 118:8 King David writes, 'It is better to take refuge in the LORD than to trust in man.' Where do we take refuge? In the arms of the Lord or in man? This is our starting point. This is our starting point in terms of living as Christians and, I believe crucially, in our marriages. As born again believers, we are aware of our sinful disposition, which seeks to trust in self. By the saving grace of Christ, we now come to God as our Heavenly Father knowing that He loves, cares and protects us … perfectly. God is the absolute expression of perfect. His being, His ways, are higher, greater, bigger, wider, deeper than anything else by far. He is One that we can completely and utterly rely on and trust even in the times that we do not understand and in things we cannot see. This is a huge point in relation to the times of trial that Christians face, and it is of huge significance in human relationships. We have a God we can rely on, we have a Saviour who has died for us, and the promised Counsellor, the Holy Spirit, who is now with us by faith in Christ's saving blood. This is truth that we see throughout Scripture (Psalm 56:3, Isaiah 43:2).

As Christians, we can joyfully seek to take refuge in the Lord and trust in Him. Therefore, for single people, people in relationships, even married people, it is imperative to understand that our hope, our security, our very identity is found only in our Lord and not in any human relationship. As a result, the means by which I am, or any man or woman is, 'untrustworthy' in and of themselves is not the damning poison that will ultimately define a marriage. Rather, it is the sin that your Saviour has defeated at Calvary and is putting to death in your life of sanctification (Romans 8:13). When we get *this,* we get real and we are Biblically equipped to develop genuine, heartfelt trust in our marriages.

When I made it clear to my wife that in and of myself I cannot be trusted, this is not a means of destabilising the base of our marriage, but a means of establishing what our base actually is! Unfortunately, my wife cannot trust me to always put her needs before my own. She cannot always rely upon me to love her in the way that Scripture commands as I will fall victim to the temptations of lust, anger, resentment and much more. And yet, she can trust the Saviour who is at work in me. She can trust the Saviour who has saved me. She can trust the Saviour who is doing a mighty sanctifying work in me. Therefore, it is not only right, but necessary, to say that a husband should trust his wife and a wife should trust her husband. This is because we do not stand 'in and of ourselves'. We stand in the righteousness of Christ, in whom we have our identity and although we may still falter and fail, our Saviour has won the war over sin and death and we stand on the victory side. It is incredible and beautiful to see the impact that Christ's saving blood has upon not only the heart of the individual but upon relationships too. And yet we realise, and maybe are thinking right now about, the many ways by which our spouse is failing and where trust is so difficult even in a supposed 'Christian' marriage. Therefore, let's explore some crucial steps to building Biblical, Christ-centred trust between a husband and wife.

1. Realism

The Lord Jesus very clearly states in Mark 14:38, 'Watch and pray that you may not enter into temptation. The spirit indeed is willing, but the flesh is weak.'

Wives, your husbands are not perfect. Husbands, your wives are not perfect! Therefore, in a marriage, we cannot aim to conceal for the sake of a 'stronger marriage'. You may think, *'If my wife knew how easily I stare at other women on the street, if my wife knew how angry she makes me when she asks me to help around the house, if my wife knew how much I drink when I am out, then she would think I am awful.'*

The cross of Christ exposes your heart and it exposes your sin. Because of His saving grace, you are declared righteous in the eyes of God, but you are still prone to these sinful feelings. This is the reality for every single Christian! We cannot pretend to be anything else especially in our marriages with a person who knows you intimately. You are 'one flesh' which means in the good and the bad, in strength and in weakness. You cannot uphold a standard of apparent perfection because it is a lie and it means that you clothe yourself with an attitude of the Pharisees in the time of Christ's life on earth. They lived a religious life where they acted in a way that was inconsistent with the heart. Do you really want to be that type of husband or wife? This is inconsistent with your existence as a Christian. The Christian life is the admission that you are a weak sinner and in need of grace every day of your life. Husband, in your sense of pride and power as the 'man' of the house, you fail instantly when you create an image of such *manliness* which suggests you are not struggling and battling against sin and its effects. You, like your wife, must expose the reality of your struggles to your wife. The Bible is clear that you are a sinner and still battling sin. Do not pretend anything else! It is sin that makes trust so difficult in a marriage, but to 'sweep it under the rug' creates a superficial trust at best, which is even more damaging on a long-term basis. It is, rather, by exposing your weakness and struggles to your spouse that trust can be built.

2. Communication

I have a vivid memory of watching an older couple sitting 'together' in a restaurant. It must have been at least a quarter of an hour until I saw them say anything to each other—and that was brief!

There is also the other extreme of couples talking and talking and getting to the heart of absolutely nothing in each other's lives! It is very easy and pointless to formulate a relationship that focuses on the weather, sport and many other superficial topics. That is not to belittle such conversations but it cannot become a 'smoke screen' for getting to what really matters. Communication is a necessity in marriage particularly in terms of building Christ-centred trust, but that comes by communicating constantly and from the heart. But we must be clear and state that proper communication is uncomfortable even with your spouse! There are things we feel are better left *unsaid* and that would 'make life a lot easier'. This is not to say that open communication that leads to more arguments and tension is a positive thing, but it is the result of something positive and gives a greater grounding for establishing genuine trust in a marriage.

In my life, if I am to trust a person, I need to know a person. In addition to this, when I know a person and know the reasons why they are not be trusted, we then need to come to the One in whom we can trust to fix that! In marriage, this is what a husband and wife actively seek to do together and so must communicate.

3. Support

This then takes us very appropriately to the crucial objective in realism and communication in a marriage, namely that you are working together to support each other. On that basis we must realise that we are all 'being made beautiful' by our bridegroom Jesus Christ. In our marriages on this earth, we are fighting for each other for that end! It is then helpful to picture a marriage relationship as two people looking towards Jesus, seeking to be like Him. When it becomes about Jesus, the desire to sin is being graciously destroyed, and greater becomes the willingness to fight sin. An intimate 'one flesh' relationship requires a realistic base and understanding of each other's sins, and a readiness to fight for each other, even carrying each other's burdens for the sake of the Lord and for your marriage.

In Romans 13:14 Paul writes, 'But put on the Lord Jesus Christ, and make no provision for the flesh, to gratify its desires.'

So what practical steps should be taken?

The most important thing to do is to ensure that time is routinely and intentionally given to talk and to pray before the Lord. Husbands, this is something that you should be initiating as the head of the marriage! It is a pitiful sight when a man is slumped by the television and his wife is pleading with him that they talk together about more than 'who's winning the match'.

I can offer no golden insight into the benefit of this except to state the obvious. When we spend time with a person we build something. Time with our spouse, time together with our God, that is precious. And inevitably, and wonderfully, it is the means of building trust.

In my marriage, I have deemed it necessary on many an occasion to speak with Binglin about how she is doing spiritually, if she has any struggles, and equally sharing my own thoughts and feelings. This is good practice and yet I believe I should have made this a more routine, habitual part of our weekly (and even daily) communication. It has been such a formative part of the building of trust to take time to sit down together and be open with each other, and when we don't have the answers or feel very low or upset, just to come to God in prayer. Laying those burdens, those worries, at the foot of the cross and praying that the

Holy Spirit would continue to do a mighty work in our individual lives and in our marriage.

In this way of communicating, Binglin and I make ourselves more vulnerable before each other in a way that is protected by the knowledge that our ultimate submission is to Christ.

Broken trust?
Another important aspect of the topic of 'trust' in marriage is that of broken trust. There are sadly many examples of trust that has been built or 'readily given' in marriage and then it is broken by a significant betrayal or series of actions. So what if you just can't trust your spouse? She has been intimate with another man? He has been verbally abusive? What then?

Let me highlight a number of key points here and I would stress that such a process will likely require the involvement of church leaders, or an older trusted Christian couple, to support in such areas of counselling.

1. Is your spouse a believer?
This may seem like a ridiculous question, but sadly it is a necessary starting point. In certain cases, where a man or woman has possibly been violent or abusive or has had an adulterous affair, such actions are blatant sins and offences to the Living God. In a marital counselling situation that my wife and I were involved in, it became very clear that the husband was not a believer, despite professing faith prior to and on the day of his wedding.

This question is an important starting point because the answer to the question will then determine the course of action. If your spouse has broken your trust and it becomes apparent that he/she is not a believer, then the need for repentance and faith in Jesus Christ as Lord and Saviour is the priority. The sin that has led to the broken trust becomes the platform to articulate the need for this man to get right with God by coming to Christ in saving faith. If God graciously saves, then this is the glorious foundation for genuine change of the heart and the basis upon which reconciliation can be reached.

However, if your spouse is a believer, then a different approach is required and the following points become more relevant and applicable.

2. Discuss clearly what has happened

This point will require another examination of Chapter 3 (Blame) because this is not an invitation to simply berate your spouse … no matter how deserving they are! It is crucial to talk through what has happened and work your way back as far as is necessary. For example, if your husband has been gambling for three months, then it may be necessary to work your way back a further six months to establish the triggers and the heart problems that led to this. Another important consideration is realising any way in which you have contributed to the circumstances. If your spouse has hurt you and broken your trust then this can be disappointing, and at times even devastating, but before addressing the issue it is crucial to clearly establish as much of the facts and history as possible, and that is likely to include the ways in which you have sinned.

3. Confession of sin

If your spouse has done something/much to break your trust, then it is important that he/she realises this and confesses their sins (1 John 1:9). It will bear little fruit for you to state their wrongdoing if they do not see this, and truly from their heart. This is why a superficial apology is but mere empty words and why actions will often be the fruit of a heartfelt apology. Nevertheless, when your spouse realises the way by which he/she has hurt you, this will be clearly articulated with a heart and posture of repentance before God and towards yourself.

In marriages which have broken down, this is a significant step towards reconciliation. It is also necessary that you have a desire to work towards reconciliation, not because your spouse deserves it, but because we have already been richly blessed by the reconciliation of Christ's saving blood on the cross. This is undoubtedly where any couple in the face of great troubles such as broken trust must seek to joyfully fight for their marriages.

However, even if you get to the stage where your spouse has confessed their sins and asked for your forgiveness, how can you trust them again?

4. *Only God can change the heart*

This sub-topic of 'broken trust' is not completely detached from the earlier parts of this Chapter. Therefore, much of what has already been written applies at this point. However, it is important to realise that when something is done that breaks what trust is there, it is a very fragile thing. For example, a porcelain ornament is already a delicate item and once it has been dropped and broken it becomes all the more fragile! Those cracks are there and they won't go away. This is the reality of the lives of broken sinners and the reality of broken relationships on this earth. It requires a greater cleaving on the part of the hurt/broken person to Christ in order to have a forgiving heart towards their spouse and a willingness to fight for the marriage and risk making themselves vulnerable. It is true that if a person has hurt you and betrayed your trust that it is more difficult to move forward. It is also true to state that such a person is more likely to betray that trust again. These are difficulties that cannot go away. Yet this is exactly what our Lord has in His dealings with us, broken and fallen people. We have been forgiven and are being restored, yet we continue to sin against Him, to hurt Him, to do things that are not in keeping with that of 'the bride of Christ'. It is therefore only God who can change the heart of His bride, and thus, only God who can and does change the hearts of husbands/wives who have caused much hurt to break trusts in marriages. God is doing a mighty sanctifying work in each of us and that is the foundation for our hope. That is the basis by which a marriage can truly go on and move forward in strength. I am so thankful for this. I am so thankful for what my Saviour has done, is doing and will continue to do graciously in my life and in the life of my spouse. That does not make marriage easy, that does not make trust easy, but it makes it possible, it makes it realistic, because of His grace and mercy to us.

5

SEXUAL PURITY

WHEN I WAS 12 years old, I was very excited about a school day trip to Alton Towers at the end of my first year at High School. We were taking an overnight bus from Aberdeenshire all the way to the Midlands in England so it promised to be a long journey! The journey started with much excitement, singing and shouting before requests were made to the teachers who organised the trip to watch some films that they had brought. What film would young teenagers request to watch in the late 1990s? American Pie. I had heard of this film but knew little about it, and I am glad that I didn't watch the film avidly on this bus journey ... but I saw enough! If we can set aside the complete lunacy of this film being permitted on a school trip, the overall premise of this film encapsulates much of our culture regarding the topic of sex, namely, *you are teenager and your next life objective is to lose your virginity.* As you read this, does that shock you? Or is it 'par for the course' given the culture in which you live? On a similar note, I remember watching a sitcom in which two males characters labelled their friend a 'freak' for only having had a sexual relationship with one woman. In Western society sexual intimacy has become about the 'experience', and the quality of the physical act of sex has become the 'ideal' leading to much frustration if this is not found. In addition, seemingly everything that is advertised uses sexualised images and content all the way from a brand new sports car to an ice cream, as well as magazines, television and internet being rife with sexualised content. And for any average young person it is considered 'normal' to have many sexual partners and to have sexual intercourse and live with your partner long before you even consider marriage.

It is a startling reality that in many churches today there is a distinct lack of Biblical teaching on this topic. Many young churchgoers and professing Christians have a lack of understanding of the importance of sexual intimacy and what that should look like Biblically, and the numbers of church-going people in sexual relationships outside of marriage are increasingly and alarmingly high! Therefore, we are going to think about the importance and beauty of sexual intimacy solely between a husband a wife in this Chapter and in the subsequent Chapter there will be careful attention given to the dangers of lust within marriage.

Satan's deception

> Now the serpent was more crafty than any other beast of the field that the Lord God had made. He said to the woman, 'Did God actually say, "You shall not eat of any tree in the garden"?' And the woman said to the serpent, 'We may eat of the fruit of the trees in the garden, but God said, "You shall not eat of the fruit of the tree that is in the midst of the garden, neither shall you touch it, lest you die."' But the serpent said to the woman, 'You will not surely die. For God knows that when you eat of it your eyes will be opened, and you will be like God, knowing good and evil' (Genesis 3:1-5).

There is much that can be unpacked from this passage, but let us draw out one very significant point. Satan appears for the first time in Scripture in the form of a serpent (John 8:44) and he goes on the offensive. Satan attacks God's designed order by targeting the female. He questions the very commands of the Living God and he lies in a very cunning way. It is the cunning way in which he lies that we will consider here.

However, when you study the serpent's communication in this passage, he is not *simply* lying. His assertion *'You will not surely die'* is very much a lie, but it is disguised and worded with truth. His approach is initially to question God's command, 'Did God actually say …' This is a clever and vindictive way of instigating doubt and uncertainty in the mind of the *then* sinless woman. When the woman responds, the serpent then lies, but he has created a foundation for his lie. The condition of man dying is disobedience against God, by eating the fruit that is forbidden, but Satan turns this into something else. Notice his response. He says, *'You will not surely die. For God knows that when you eat of it your eyes will be opened, and you will be like God, knowing good and evil.'* What has he done here? He has turned the eating of the fruit into something positive and tried to 'turn the tables' on God's command. He is in effect saying, 'God is holding something back.' 'You are losing out.' On one mistaken level, there is truth in this, because if the man and woman eat the fruit, then they will 'be like God' in regards to then knowing good and evil. However, the serpent has not revealed the means by which that is achieved which is to disobey God and destroy the perfect image of the Living God! Satan has cunningly deceived her to turn sin into something so desirable. He has achieved this by planting the seed of doubt into the mind of the woman, not by trying to accuse God with an outright lie, but trying to create in the heart and mind of the woman the notion that she is losing out on something by not eating the fruit. This is undoubtedly a lie, but it is a clever lie. This is the tactic of the master of lies and it is a tactic used ever since to attack humanity.

The abuse of God's gift of sexual intimacy
As we reflected on our study in Genesis 2 (see Chapter 1) the physical consummation of a marriage is a beautiful gift of the Lord in which one man and woman can enjoy the unique physical togetherness of being 'one flesh'. Sexual union is encouraged and commanded in Scripture—only between a man and a woman who are joined together in marriage. This is God's design and it

is beautiful, it is right ... and it is radically counter-cultural in Western society. And Satan has taken that beautiful design of the Lord and he has tried to destroy and often successfully destroyed it in the lives of many people.

Back in Genesis 3, the pattern of deception is made clear and it is very much the way in which Satan targets and tries to destroy sexual purity in the lives of many, even born again believers. Satan will come to the unmarried single person and dating couple, and make them think that they are missing out on something. In a similar fashion to Genesis 3, *'Did God actually say that? You are missing out on something beautiful that God has created. Sex is a beautiful thing.'* That's positive, right? Sex is a gift from God. That's true. Yet we can see clearly how Satan has distorted the truth. He is the master of deception. Adding to that, as a result of the Fall we are now battling against unhealthy and ungodly sexual desires. We may then ask why we have to wait until we are married? If two people love each other then is there really a problem?

The simple response is that it is unbiblical and goes against the command and design of the Lord. However, let's unpack why this is the case. Although Satan may have 'sugar coated' the lie of sexual intimacy outwith marriage, what he has not revealed to you is that when you willingly give yourself in the most intimate of ways with a man or woman that is not your spouse, you are coming together with a person who the very next day could say 'SEE YOU LATER' and it's over. There are no guarantees, but instead there is fear, worry and insecurity. Even a loving relationship is not a stronghold in the face of this, particularly as it is a direct disobedience against the Most High God! And our Great God cares and loves His children too much to have a 'pleasure now, think and suffer later' mentality. This is why a man or woman is given the blessing of being at their most vulnerable within the framework of a marriage relationship where the marriage bed becomes the beautiful expression of something glorious that God has done!

Sex is not about the 'experience'

Another damaging lie of Satan is the tragic distortion of sex as an experience that is defined by its quality. In secular society, a sexual encounter is often analysed based on the answers to questions such as, 'How good was he?' and 'Was it the best yet?'

For the unmarried Christian, the danger is clear. If sex is defined by these terms, then the notion of one partner is not only limiting, but it is a gamble. 'What if your spouse is *no good?*' Human beings like variety, they like quality, and this is the framework according to which a good sexual experience seems like a 'right and fun' way to live.

Let's be abundantly clear to state that such thinking for the Bible-believing Christian is a complete contradiction in terms. The desire that man has for the 'best possible experience' is a direct result of the Fall where man seeks to serve himself for his own glory. As you are confronted with and convicted by your sin, you repent of your sin and believe in Jesus Christ as your Lord and Saviour. In this, your desire, your purpose, your hope and your joy is now built upon and for the God that you worship and the God for whom you were made. Therefore, sex, like everything else, becomes a God-centred issue. The secular world, at enmity with God, promoting sex on the basis of experience, variety and quality is for the sake of serving the fallen sinner who does not know God. By the grace of God, the Christian is aware of this lie. Therefore, positive feelings are not the basis for our joy, but truth is the basis. Our feelings do matter, but on the basis of the truth of God's Word, living for His Glory. Therefore, the pleasure and joy of sex is within that framework because this is what God has designed. This is not to say that we are to go to extremes of suggesting that the Christian should not enjoy sex or spend time thinking about their sex life, but rather, to say that such thinking must be defined and driven by Scripture and not by the world.

Union with Christ

It must be stressed that a person is not 'unfulfilled' or 'incomplete' if they do not have a sexual relationship. If this were true, then what would we say of the Apostle Paul? And deeper still, of the only perfect man who ever lived, the Lord Jesus Christ? Therefore, we must grasp that any notion that we can be more complete, happier or satisfied with a sexual relationship is a great lie of Satan.

We can give thanks to the Lord that He graciously exposes the forgiven sinner to this lie and our absolute need for Christ. It is in Christ, and Christ alone, that one can have true, genuine and full satisfaction. This is because it is in Christ that we are completely exposed to our 'sinful baggage' and are cleansed. Therefore, if you are reading this Chapter as someone who has committed sexual acts even as a 'backsliding believer', there may be emotional scars as a result of this, but there is not ultimate condemnation when we come to Christ in repentance and saving faith. As we saw in Ephesians 5:26, Christ is cleansing His bride. For every born again believer, we are that bride, we are the church! That is amazing! This the perfect union, the perfect intimacy that we all enjoy fully and joyfully. And *this* is what must be our focal point when discussing sexual purity.

Perhaps you are asking, or are trying to counsel someone asking questions such as this: *Must I stop sleeping with my partner? Can I live with my partner? Can I have a relationship with someone of my own sex?* Before responding to such questions, the most important question must be: Are you right with God? Have you entered into the only perfect and intimate relationship that sinful man can have which is with the Lord Jesus Christ? It is by understanding and believing in Christ that we are aware of our sin and are being cleansed of our sin. It is that relationship with Christ that can truly satisfy the soul.

Sex within marriage

And God blessed them. And God said to them, 'Be fruitful and multiply and fill the earth and subdue it, and have dominion over the fish of the sea and over the birds of the heavens and over every living thing that moves on the earth' (Genesis 1:28).

> Let marriage be held in honour among all, and let the marriage bed be undefiled, for God will judge the sexually immoral and adulterous (Hebrews 13:4).

Sexual intimacy is not simply encouraged but it is commanded in Scripture ... to married couples. In certain Christian circles, any talk of sex is considered 'taboo' as a means of almost recoiling at the way the world has distorted sex. However, it is right and Biblical to stress that sex is not simply 'OK' for married couples, but it is a blessing from God. Below are three key ways by which married couples can and should enjoy their sexual union in a pure and right way as two sinners who have been forgiven by grace and find full and eternal satisfaction and joy in their bridegroom, the Lord Jesus Christ.

1. Unique expression of togetherness

I was counselling a young man who was confused about the difference between the relationship of a married couple and two close friends. Inevitably I stressed the importance of God's institution of marriage and the covenant relationship, which is binding as a man and a woman become 'one flesh'. In 1 Corinthians 6, the Apostle Paul is warning against sexual immorality and in verse 16 we read, 'Or do you not know that he who is joined to a prostitute becomes one body with her? For, as it is written, "The two will become one flesh."'

What is striking here is the significance placed upon the sexual relationship. Even in the case of a man lying with a prostitute we read that he becomes 'one body with her'. That is a weighty phrase and is emphasised by the reminder that two people who 'come together' become 'one flesh'. This is a direct reference to the institution of marriage in Genesis 2:24 and this gives central emphasis to the sexual relations as a means of sealing this 'oneness'. Therefore, unlike in any other relationship, a husband and a wife have a special, God-given means by which they seal their union by entering into a sexual relationship, which is thus a unique expression of that togetherness.

Do you see how markedly different this definition and understanding of sexual union is in comparison to the teaching and emphasis of the world? Sex is belittled into some kind of sport where the coming together with another in such an intimate way is often merely 'physical' and for the sake of 'experience'. In marriage, our very bodies belong to one another (1 Corinthians 7:4) and there is something far deeper about the physical union of a sexual relationship between a husband and a wife where one can be at their most physically and emotionally vulnerable with the one to whom you are bound by the grace and purpose of the Living God. When you give yourself to your husband or wife in marriage, you are giving 'all' of yourself. We know this is true based on the teachings of Genesis 2 and Ephesians 5. A husband and a wife become 'one flesh'. They enter into a covenant relationship that is instituted by the Lord. The marriage relationship is a visible picture of the binding union between Christ and His church, one that cannot and will not be broken. This binding, life-long togetherness is therefore a glorious God-given context in which sexual desires cannot simply be satisfied but they can be expressed freely and joyfully.

2. Procreation

In Genesis 1:28 we read, 'And God blessed them. And God said to them, "Be fruitful and multiply and fill the earth and subdue it, and have dominion over the fish of the sea and over the birds of the heavens and over every living thing that moves on the earth."'

God has ordained that the beautiful gift of children is wrought by the sexual relations of a man and a woman in marriage. We see at the beginning of God's Word that God's very first words, His first command to mankind is to 'Be fruitful and multiply'. This is the means by which the earth is to be populated and the Bible is clear that children are a blessing from the Lord: 'Behold, children are a heritage from the Lord, the fruit of the womb a reward' (Psalm 127:3).

The challenge and importance of children will be covered in Chapter 8, but it is necessary to identify here that children are a blessing from the Lord and this is a blessed result of the physical togetherness a husband and wife enjoy as 'one flesh'.

3. Fulfilling sexual desires

It is potentially contentious to state that sexual relationships are also a means of fulfilling sexual desires, true though this may be. In 1 Corinthians 7:5 we read, 'Do not deprive one another, except perhaps by agreement for a limited time, that you may devote yourselves to prayer; but then come together again, so that Satan may not tempt you because of your lack of self-control.'

But we ask, what of the single person? The Apostle Paul helps us here in regards to a number of issues, this one included, in Philippians 4:12-13, 'I know how to be brought low, and I know how to abound. In any and every circumstance, I have learned the secret of facing plenty and hunger, abundance and need. I can do all things through him who strengthens me.'

Sexual desires are a natural part of a human being and it is therefore a blessing for one's desires to be fulfilled. However, they must not be fulfilled at the expense of our holiness and the Glory of God. If that were the case, then our sexual satisfaction would be of the utmost priority in our lives, as it may be for many who are 'of the world'. Yet, in Christ, our absolute satisfaction and contentment is in Christ Jesus and Paul learns that in any situation when even faced with hunger, he knows he can do all things in the strength of Jesus Christ! This is why our ultimate need and satisfaction is in Christ.

Therefore, there is not a *necessity* for sexual relations in our lives, but as we see in 1 Corinthians 7:5, sexual relations within marriage is the means of fulfilling sexual desires and this should be done and enjoyed. That enjoyment is not based on a 10/10 performance but upon the realisation you are with your spouse! You can make mistakes, you are safe, you can express yourself in a way where you are comfortable.

There is a great responsibility within the local church, led by her leadership, in teaching and guiding the flock to a Biblical understanding of sexual purity within marriage and the importance of celibacy outwith marriage.

When I firmly said 'NO' to my daughter when she put her fingers into the electrical socket, I was not acting as a 'fun police officer' but as a source of protection and safety. This applies in regards to the topic of sex, but more than that, the Scriptures make clear the way by which sexual intimacy can be enjoyed and fulfilled between a husband and a wife within a marriage. It must also be reiterated that though sexual relations are a blessing, they are not the means of ultimate satisfaction. For the single person or the married person, our ultimate satisfaction is only and fully found in Christ. This must be grasped, period. And in relation to this topic, this is our starting point and foundation that we be guarded against the desire to enter into sexual immorality and that we may be able to enjoy sexual intimacy in its proper God-given context within marriage.

6

LUST

An issue of the heart

PERMIT ME TO paint a realistic picture. It's evening time and your spouse is out with some friends for the night. You've had a tiring day and frivolously getting through the evening, doing very little. You're now sitting at the computer 'surfing the internet', casually looking at social media amidst other sites. You then notice a thumbnail with a rather attractive immodestly dressed member of the opposite sex. At *this* point you are at war! You are at war with that voice of temptation, guided by Satan, which is telling you, *'Wow, that's nice, go and have a quick look … it's not a big deal … because nobody will even know!'* This is a battle in your heart for purity (Matthew 5:8). Is this evidence of how weak your love and commitment to your spouse is? Does this show that you are a sexual sinner? What's going on?

The teaching of the Lord Jesus in the Sermon on the Mount is a significant and potent challenge in defining and applying the dangers of 'lust', not simply in a marriage but in the life of any Christian. In Matthew 5:27-30 we read,

You have heard that it was said, 'You shall not commit adultery.' But I say to you that everyone who looks at a woman with lustful intent has already committed adultery with her in his heart. If your right eye causes you to sin, tear it out and throw it away. For it is better that you lose one of your members than that your whole body be thrown into hell. And if your right hand causes you to sin, cut it off and throw it away. For it is better that you lose one of your members than that your whole body go into hell.

Jesus was preaching at a time when the Religious leaders had formed a legalistic standard that could account for their own self-righteousness based upon their own traditions and interpretations of the law. This meant that one's sexual purity was defined by whether or not they had physically committed the act of adultery. If they had not, they would be considered righteous by upholding the seventh commandment (Exodus 20:14). As we study Jesus' teaching in the Sermon on the Mount, is He then *changing* or *adding* to the law in passages like Matthew 5:27-30? Absolutely not. Jesus is condemning the misinterpretation of the law by the Religious leaders. The key difference here is that the basis of one's righteousness is not by keeping the 'letter' of the law on an external level. The Scriptures are clear that no-one is righteous (Romans 3:10) and that one must be born again (John 3:3) in order to be declared righteous in the eyes of the Lord. Therefore, the Lord Jesus gives very practical teaching, consequently condemning the misinterpretation of the law by the Religious leaders, teaching which addresses the heart. This is a sermon that Jesus preached to enable Christians to know how to live as followers of their Saviour and so He addresses the issue of the heart, again and again.

Let's be realistic now. We can create an image of sexual purity (and loyalty to our spouse) if the definition is based on the outward action. Perhaps you have never committed the physical act of adultery, and if *that* is the standard of righteousness and sexual purity in marriage then we can just ignore this Chapter. And yet, if this is how we seek to practically live as Christians then it means that we do not understand the Gospel. The Gospel is the Good News that Jesus Christ died for unworthy sinners, not to prove how indispensable we are, but to show how serious our sin is. When a sinner comes in repentance and saving faith, the entire heart is transformed from one that seeks to live for self and now for the Glory of the Lord. This must be stressed at this point because though we 'whole-heartedly' agree in theory, is this how we live in practice?

Are you open to talk about your struggles in the area of sexual sin? Do you justify such a topic on the basis of: *'Well, I don't act on it'*?

I may have a 'happier' marriage *externally* by concealing my real struggles in this area, but this is not only dishonest, but it is inconsistent with the teachings of Jesus Christ and what it means to be a Christian. The cross of Christ is not a spiritual booster to improve the 'already pretty good you'. In Matthew 5:28 the Lord Jesus is abundantly clear; to simply *look* at a woman lustfully is adultery in the heart. This is an internal, heart issue. When any one of us is tempted to take that second look at the woman running on the beach or that man exercising at the gym, or at that pop up ad that you didn't go looking for on your computer screen, this is the spiritual war that we face in our battle against lust. It does not have to result in addictions to pornography (although this is a problem for Christians too) or physical acts with a man or woman outside of marriage, because simply watching these videos, looking at these men or women, they create the thoughts and the temptations in the heart and mind.

Our questions at the start: Is this evidence of how weak your love and commitment to your spouse is? Does this show that you are a sexual sinner? What's going on? What's going on is that you are a sinner in need of Christ. Sexual temptation is real and dangerous and nobody is immune. Let me be clear here that no matter how much you love your spouse or how amazing you think they are or how amazing you claim to be as a born again believer, you cannot guarantee the right victory in this battle (and it is a battle for everyone in different ways) every time on your own! You could be a woman who adores her husband and think he's the most gorgeous guy on the planet, and the most amazing man ever. But this is not enough! We are sinfully wired, and the mind can manipulate our deeper feelings at times. We are still susceptible. I am truly thankful that the Lord Jesus has such an intimate care for my spiritual growth that He diagnoses this problem and gives us very clear commands in the face of such sinful struggles.

Cut it out
When we read Jesus' definition of adultery in the heart, do we have an unattainable standard for us to follow?

In response to this question, we must remind ourselves of the spiritual condition of the forgiven sinner. Our righteousness is not based upon perfect obedience to the law, for that is an unattainable standard for sinful man. Our righteousness is based upon the perfect obedience of Christ to death on a cross (Philippians 2:8), which is imputed to us. This does not mean that we must perfectly obey the teachings *in order to be saved,* but because we have been saved by Christ and stand in His righteousness, we seek to obey His teachings as His disciples. Therefore, we have an unattainable standard if this is the requirement for salvation, but it is not. This means that a more relevant question should be *how* we fight for our sexual purity in light of and in obedience to Jesus' teaching in this passage. As married couples, how do we fight against the temptations we face in our heart when using the internet, and in magazines, on posters, on our streets?

Again we must stress the importance of being realistic about the limitations and struggles of our spouse. This is a huge point in this area! Let me explain what this does *not* mean.

First of all this does not mean that you readily accept that your spouse is a sinner who has a tendency to sin, and stop there. You accept, rather, that your spouse is a sinner who must be willing to take the relevant action, with your support and prayers, to fight against this sin! It is therefore wholly unhelpful if a man is open about his struggles for the sake of his holiness and to be a better husband, and the wife responds by chastising him for not being a man, for being weak and pathetic, and not 'living like a Christian'. If a man is willing to talk openly about his struggles (and he should!), then he is doing it because he has a desire to fight against his sin getting bigger. He is fighting for the sake of his holiness. So, wives, fight with him! Husbands, fight for her! Fight for him! Is this easy? Is it easy to share about your own struggles or to hear about the struggles of your spouse? No, it is not. This is why we must fight for our marriages. This is the fight that married couples tackle 'head on' at the source. If a man or a woman is already at a stage where he/she is addicted to pornography, flirting with other people or worse, then you are already way down a line where you start fighting a losing battle. Therefore, it is crucial to see that this is a fight against the source of temptation that can lead to sexual sin that can spiral out of control.

We can then look back to the practical application of the Lord Jesus in Matthew 5:29-30. The teaching of Christ is not simply relevant for couples fighting in their marriages, but for anyone fighting in the face of lust. So what does Jesus go on to say in verses 29-30? He uses strong imagery to effectively tell us that if something tempts us, cut it out! If your right eye causes you to sin, gouge it out, or your right hand causes you to sin, cut it off. That's not a literal teaching but rather a picture of cutting out these potential temptations and struggles. Therefore, if the internet keeps getting you down, seriously, cut it out. It does not matter if you *need* the internet or your phone, or anything else in today's day and age, because nothing is worth more than your holiness and purity before Christ and in your marriages! Jesus is very clear and to the point—cut it out! We are sinful people who are prone to sin so do not let the devil get a foothold, do not even smell the chocolate cake because you are simply feeding the desire to devour it.

This practical application that our Lord gives to us must be seriously applied in the face of the 'as long as …' argument. For example, I may argue with myself that it is OK to watch a film that has immodestly dressed women, or a film that has sexualised content *as long as there is no nudity.* This sort of thinking is a problem. Jesus does not say, 'as long as …' in response to the dangers of lust. He states very clearly that we are to cut it out! You may then argue that it's OK if it is something that doesn't tempt you? I may think that a 'sex scene' isn't a source of tempta-tion for me because I don't find the actress physically attractive. Again, we must not give the devil a foothold (Ephesians 4:27). Even if you do not go 'looking for it' and even though it may not be something you think is tempting to you, we must seek to approach this entire area with the 'cut it out' mindset. If some-thing has the potential to cause us to stumble or to tempt us then it is absolutely best and right to avoid it, to cut it out. If we try to dance near the edge of temptation then it becomes all the more straightforward for Satan to devour us. You must remember, even if you are living in such a morally upright and pure way, it just takes a few seconds for you to stumble and spiral into the pit of temptation, lust and more.

For every married couple, therefore, the realism that must be considered is that we live in a sinful world, a sinfully sexualised world, and our purity is not defined primarily by our outward actions. It is the issue of the heart that our Lord Jesus addresses in this passage and this is where we must go in our communication and in our prayers as we fight for our sexual purity in marriage. We are not immune to sexual temptation, regardless of age, stage, background or track record. We must be serious in the face of this fight and as has already been stated, couples must take this fight on together. It is not a denial of the love you have for your spouse to be open about your struggles, but rather, a means of seeking to strengthen it. We are weak and prone to sin in and of ourselves, but as Christians we now have One who is fighting for us who has already conquered sin and death and its effects. Therefore, we come to Christ in repentance and cleave to Him as we seek to grow with Him. It is in looking to Christ that any individual and every couple can become more like Him and move further away from even the 'desires' of sexual sin. I am utterly convinced upon the authority of God's Word that the fight against sexual sin must be tackled from the source. It is essential that we seek to tackle and cut out temptation from the beginning by treating it like a cancer. As soon as it is found and diagnosed, action is taken so that it does not spread, getting worse and thus lead to irreparable and potentially incurable damage. This is how serious sexual sin is if left unattended in our hearts because it is from that point that a simple 'look' can become a consistent look, to an addiction, to a physical action and more.

Practical Questions
Temptation is a monumental battle in any marriage on a range of issues and the topic of lust is very much one of the greatest battles. In addition to what we have considered in this Chapter, permit me to pose two practical questions in conclusion:

- Is this source of temptation, and all its sexual beauty and pleasure as beautiful and as precious and pleasurable as the Glory of God, as the Saviour whose sweet embrace you have felt by His blood-stained arms stretched out at the cross?

- Is this source of temptation, and all its sexual beauty and pleasure as beautiful and as precious and pleasurable as the beauty, both outwardly and inwardly, of your spouse?

In the context of our corporate worship with the Body of Christ, we will boldly declare the 'correct' answers to these questions, and rightly so! However, these are practical questions to ask in the heat of the moment when the battle for your holiness and purity is at its most threatening. At the point when your heart is racing and your hormones are raging because of the attractive girl or guy you see and want to look at again, this is when such questions become the necessary focal point in the battle against lust and to cut out these sources of temptation.

I have found that in my own growing relationship with the Lord Jesus, that His presence in my life and the truth of His Word is more engrained in my heart and at the forefront of my mind. It therefore becomes crucial for every individual and every married couple to see that when they expose themselves to the Lord, in His Word, in prayer, in fellowship, they are building a relationship with the One who has conquered sin and its effects. In this great and lasting hope that we have in our salvation, we have the Saviour who is interceding for us, the One who is fighting for us. Draw near to Him and He will be the stronger desire and presence in the face of temptation!

Flowing from that relationship with our Lord, we must obviously ask the question in the face of the temptation to have such lustful thoughts. Is it worth it? How pathetic am I, are you, that you would entertain something so cheap and filthy even in your mind instead of taking your heart to the love of a relationship with your beautiful spouse whom you treasure so much, someone who is such a precious gift from God? To spend time watching that video, or entertaining that thought, that is lust, and it is against God and your spouse! Your spouse, the one who you have possibly shared more with than anyone else, possibly the father or mother of your child, the one that you fell in love with, a love that has grown and matured, someone you are safe with in their arms, someone that you can trust and depend on, someone who has a physical beauty and an inward beauty that is like no other person. Focus your heart and your mind on that person, married husband or wife, when you face that time of temptation and possible lust, and you do so in the strength, love and togetherness you have with the God who gives you such strength that you love so passionately. Be sure to communicate this regularly and affectionately to your spouse because marriage is more than a fight against sin as forgiven sinners, restored by the blood of Christ and united in a unique and precious life-long covenant together.

The slippery slope
I have been deeply saddened by the shockingly high percentages of professing Christians who have significantly stumbled in areas of sexual sin. High profile pastors exposed as having adulterous relationships, professing Christians in sexual relationships

outside marriage, sexual addictions to pornography and much more. I have seen some statistics stating that 50, 60, even 70 percent of certain age groups of professing Christians are addicted to various sexual materials which they watch with some regularity. What is most frightening of all is that this is one of the most 'secret' areas of a person's life and so how much higher would the *actual* statistics be?

All of these instances are the ugly consequence of letting the initial stages of temptation and struggle fester and grow.

Does an addiction to pornography begin from day one? No! How many born again believers would suddenly start watching hardcore pornography with regularity? How many married men or women would enter into a fully-fledged sexual relationships with another person not long after meeting that person?

The teaching of our Lord Jesus in Matthew 5 on this topic is direct and it is severe for good and necessary reasons!

Permit me to unravel one of these sadly 'typical scenarios':

Janine has been married to Bob for ten years. They have two children, aged 7 and 5 and they are both at primary school. Janine has been working part-time as a receptionist. She loves her husband, they have had a fairly 'steady' marriage but have spent less time together after they have had kids and communication and the overall 'spark' has waned. At her work, many young and successful businessmen pass the reception desk and one guy, Mike, is a very friendly, warm guy. Mike always makes an effort to speak to Janine, and has even complimented how 'great' she looks for someone who has given birth. Janine begins to remember that her husband Bob used to compliment her but she hasn't heard anything like that in years!

Let's stop at this point and ask some important questions. Is Janine desperately unhappy in her marriage? No. Is Janine looking for an adulterous relationship? No. Is Janine attracted to another man apart from her husband? That's a bit more difficult! It would be fair to say that everything in this scenario is 'fine' and 'above board' on an external level. However, the Lord Jesus speaks to the heart! As soon as Janine's heart is racing faster at the sight of another man, as soon as Janine is hoping to see Mike and even to receive a compliment from him, this has to be 'cut out'. What may happen next? When Janine is at home, the fantasies may start. When Janine is intimate with her husband, does she have another man vying for her affection? The slippery slope may then continue. Janine may begin to 'justify' harmless flirting or texting someone who is after all a colleague! The further she will go into danger, the weaker she will be in the face of growing temptation.

This danger is one that no Christian is immune from. The counsel of the Lord Jesus in Matthew 5 must be carefully studied and applied. Consider the slippery slope of King David (2 Samuel 11). When he should have been leading the country in battle he was mindlessly strolling at home where he saw the temptation and gave in to the temptation, leading to a catalogue of wicked actions and evil intent. We must fight against the sin of lust at the very beginning. This is why when I see a 'seductive pop up' on the internet I draw this to my wife's attention that she would pray for my holiness and purity as we continue to think and pray about anything that could cause either one of us to stumble or be tempted. We cut it out for the sake of holiness. We draw closer to Christ in our growth in holiness.

It must also be stressed that if you or your spouse has already gone 'far down' that slippery slope then it is imperative that both on an individual level, but also as a couple, you seek spiritual guidance and Biblical counselling from the leadership of your church. When we face the reality of sexual addiction or physical acts of adultery, the pain and the heartbreak can be significant and destructive. Therefore, the practical guidelines at the end of Chapter 4 (on trust) most certainly apply. However, I pray that as followers of the Lord Jesus we will seek to arm ourselves in the face of the fight for our sexual purity by cutting it off, cutting it out from the beginning from the heart.

7

MONEY

THE AFFLUENCE OF an individual or couple practically determines or impacts upon lifestyle, luxury and comfort and for couples where finances are a struggle this can lead to great strain on a marriage. And yet you may wonder why a whole chapter is dedicated to such a topic because surely it is important not to place too great an emphasis on money and let it become an 'idol'. This is most certainly true and one of the ways to avoid this in a world where money is so instrumental in defining and shaping people's lives is to address this topic Biblically.

The purpose of your possessions
Let's consider our Scriptural base with a well-known passage in Matthew 6:19-24,

> Do not lay up for yourselves treasures on earth, where moth and rust destroy and where thieves break in and steal, but lay up for yourselves treasures in heaven, where neither moth nor rust destroys and where thieves do not break in and steal. For where your treasure is, there your heart will be also. The eye is the lamp of the body. So, if your eye is healthy, your whole

body will be full of light, but if your eye is bad, your whole body will be full of darkness. If then the light in you is darkness, how great is the darkness! No one can serve two masters, for either he will hate the one and love the other, or he will be devoted to the one and despise the other. You cannot serve God and money.

Jesus begins this passage in a very striking way by stating clearly that we are not to store up treasures on earth. And the first thing we need to see is that Jesus is *not* saying, 'Don't store up treasures'. The danger that is identified is when you store up money, possessions 'on earth'. So what does this term mean? Let's consider this by answering a very direct and practical question: do you *need* your money? Think carefully about it. If the answer is 'Yes!', then in what way is this a 'need'? To feed you and your family? To have a place to stay in and to have clothes to wear? That seems reasonable. However, let's see if any of the following have ever been described as 'needs'; a 'nice' house, a certain brand of car, a designer handbag, a bigger television, an upgraded mobile phone ... and we could continue for pages with comparable examples. Treasures 'on earth' is not a reference to the external amount which will differ on the basis of a couple's liberty of conscience, but this very much is of the heart. This is why a contrast is established between 'earthly' and 'heavenly' treasures. The former is temporary, the latter is everlasting. Externally, two people may have the exact same amount, but their hearts differ wildly. One treasures their stuff, the other treasures their God and the stuff becomes about their God. This is why the Lord Jesus poignantly states that *where your treasure is, there your heart is also* (verse 21).

As we embark on a number of very practical considerations regarding financial matters in a marriage, we must be clear about what our finances and possessions are for. The Lord Jesus is not condemning 'riches' and He is not encouraging an 'it's not important' attitude, but rather, He is teaching that the things that we possess, all that we have, belong to God. This is why the passage ends by stating that you cannot serve both God and money. In 1

Timothy 6:7 we read, '... for we brought nothing into the world, and we cannot take anything out of the world.'

I believe that it is imperative for every married couple to get this into view constantly and consistently in their everyday lives, which is what will be unpacked in this Chapter.

'One Flesh'

'Therefore a man shall leave his father and his mother and hold fast to his wife, and they shall become one flesh' (Genesis 2:24).

The teaching of a covenant relationship between husband and wife as 'one flesh' is a practical reality in all areas of marriage. I am yet to meet a Bible-believing Christian who has disputed the Scriptural reality of two becoming 'one flesh' in marriage. And yet, the practical application of being 'one flesh' can look very different, particularly in the area of finances.

Shortly before Binglin and I got married we were preparing for marriage (yes, we were looking beyond the wedding day!) we visited the bank. Why? We were discussing finances and setting up joint accounts (looking back, we did this just before we got married but I would advise that this is something to be done after you get married). The reason was because we were preparing for the Lord God Almighty joining us together in a precious and unique way where literally 'all that I had was hers and all that she had was mine'. Does this mean that if the man has £100k and the woman has £100 that this still applies? Some may argue in 'extreme cases' that there should be a safeguard in place (hence why prenuptial agreements are made). The Biblical answer is simple—yes. Despite this, it must be made clear that no legalistic parameters should be set up that every married couple must conform to. The practical reality will look different for each couple but establishing the Biblical premise and where our hearts are is essential.

The first issue that must be established is that whatever you have, large or small, belongs to God and you have been given stewardship over that. The issue of 'how much you have' then becomes a dangerous mindset if that is not qualified with regards to this being what the Lord has provided in His providence. The second issue is in understanding the nature of marriage as 'one flesh' as not being conditional but permanent. Therefore, your money, possessions and everything you have are not as precious or binding in the eyes of God. In light of this, it is not imperative that everything you have or own is in 'joint name' legally, but it ought to be in heart, and it may often be advisable in practice. Here are two considerations:

1. Trust

If you can imagine a husband, wife and two children where the husband is earning a handsome income and the wife does not have a regular income as she primarily serves the Lord as a wife and mother (Titus 2:4-5). The attitude of the husband must be that this is money that the Lord has blessed his entire family with. In such an instance, a joint bank account enforces trust because *his* salary becomes *their* money. Simply put, if you are joined together in the eyes of God then it's quite straightforward to be so in the eyes of the bank!

2. Transparency

Another practical danger with separate accounts is the lack of transparency and clarity about your financial situation. It must be deemed good practice to ensure the easiest means by which both a husband and a wife are fully aware of how much money they have as a couple, thus impacting more effectively regarding planning, budgeting and saving.

Is there an alternative argument where separate accounts/possessions is a sign of how much the couple trust each other? I personally think this is a dangerous argument as it can be more likely to tempt 'individualistic' thinking as well as rash spending and secrecy. This said, there is greater merit in the argument of 'allowance' accounts where individual spending and usage enables a husband or a wife to spend within the framework of the wider financial unity that they have. The other practical advantage here is that you can plan 'romantic' surprises for your spouse (ie. on a birthday) without their knowing!

Who organises the finances in a marriage?

It has been interesting for me to observe a growing trend in China of women 'controlling' the finances in marriages and families. This prompts an interesting question regarding who should organise the finances in a marriage. In order to address this question, let's apply the teaching of Scripture with regards to the roles of a husband and a wife in a marriage. The husband is the head of the wife (Ephesians 5:23) as the head in their marriage. This teaching is not the answer to our question explicitly but it establishes the framework. A husband who says, 'I don't know about money, leave that to the Mrs' is not being Biblical. Alternatively, a husband who says, 'I am the head and so I control the finances' may also be being unbiblical if his understanding of headship is such. So what is required?

A husband must understand his spiritual oversight. He has a responsibility to lead the family with a servant-like heart and that means making final decisions on such a basis. Financial matters are very much an integral part of this application. Consequently, it is then relevant to weigh up the practical discussions of 'who will do what'. If the wife is gifted with numbers, perhaps qualified as an accountant, then it makes sense that she would be the person in the family who organises some or all of the finances as the husband leads. The underlying issue is that matters of finances, like every other area of marriage, are in keeping with what the Scriptures teach about husbands and wives. I have seen many cases where a wife is organising the finances either because she has not understood what Biblical submission means or because the husband is indifferent, passive and lazy. It is also then likely that an unbiblical dynamic in an area such as financial handling can lead to not only financial difficulties but many other difficulties and strains in a marriage.

Financial planning

How much should we save each month? Should we budget for any long-term things? What about our tithing? Do we want to buy or rent a property?

There are endless questions that any given married couple will have regarding financial matters in their marriage. Whether you are reading this as someone thinking about or preparing to get married, or years into a marriage, planning is crucial.

The first point to make is that planning is important. I recently read a statistic that said less than two of every ten married couples know how to budget and keep track of their spending and saving. It is not an exaggeration to state that it would be unbiblical to be haphazard and disorganised with finances. Referring back to Jesus' teaching in the Sermon on the Mount (Matthew 6:19-24), one clear inference is that our money and possessions matter. An attitude of, 'I'll leave finances to the Lord' is not an attitude taught by the Lord Jesus because that becomes a smokescreen for slothfulness or other sinful actions. It is ultimately the grace of God in terms of what He blesses each couple with, but in that, there comes responsibility for the sake of the Kingdom and the wellbeing of that family. There are a number of important questions that can help with this process and here are four key ones:

1. What is your current financial situation?

As you sit down to plan your finances going forward, it's important to see what the situation currently is. For example, a couple preparing to get married ought to discuss how much money, if any, they have. In addition to this, what debts are either or both people carrying? If one or both have recently graduated from their respective universities, they may still have student loans to pay off, as well as costs of a wedding. This is the 'survey' question, the one that establishes the existing facts and situation, which will impact on amounts, and spending/saving approaches in the other questions.

2. How much should we 'give'?

It is important that we are deliberate here. There is a tendency for Christian couples to have the 'whatever is left' mindset with regards to their giving to church and ministry work. And sadly, there are also those that do it sporadically if at all!

During the time of the Mosaic law, the Israelites were obligated to give a 'tithe' which is a 10% giving of all that they owned. Today, Christians are not obligated by this percentage, but are instructed to give to the work of the Gospel (Matthew 10:10) and to the needy (Luke 3:10-11) joyfully (2 Corinthians 9:7). The ongoing adopted rule of 'giving 10%' of what you earn has been considered a sensible practical amount. I won't dispute that as wise counsel provided it is not made as a legalistic requirement. This is because we need to have already established that 100% belongs to our Lord and based on that joyful realisation ought to come a willingness and a priority to give from our bank accounts, possessions. The giving to the local church is the means by which her paid leaders can support themselves enabling the teaching, shepherding, guiding, leading, evangelising for the sake of the Gospel. This money can also be the means by which the Lord physically provides for the outreach work locally as well as global mission support and much more. Giving to the work of the Lord is a precious blessing and there can be no greater way of physically using our money!

On a practical level, regarding questions of 'how much' or 'what percent', my encouragement would be to give as much as you can! It would likely be unwise to say, 'Well, I earn £2,000 every month and I'm going to give three quarters of that to the church'. When planning and asking this question about giving, a balanced overview of all your financial responsibilities is key. Therefore, I find it helpful to initially set aside an amount to give, then establish what are the other financial commitments that my family needs to pay for and then there is room for greater added giving as opposed to luxury spending or wasting of your money.

3. What are the 'essentials'?

This next question is crucial and if couples can get this right then it will go a long way to avoiding many financial struggles in marriage. If I can give a hypothetical scenario to help tackle this:

Greg earns £1,800 per month on his full-time job. Kathy earns £700 part-time. They have two children at primary school.

They have decided to give £250 to their local church as their giving, leaving them with £2,250 to budget for. They pay £800 per month on their mortgage and another £300 on various bills. This leaves them with £1,150. They budget for food and other practical costs for a family of four, which amounts to £250, leaving them with £900. They make a decision to budget £200 'excess' for any unforeseen spends and they aim to save £500 in a long-term account. This leaves them with £200 left.

This example covers most of what would be described as 'essentials' for spending. It is imperative that the husband takes the lead in sitting down with his wife to discuss this, realising what their commitments are in order to avoid over-spending. With this in mind, having a 'spend less than you earn' policy is wise. I also believe it is unwise to consider satellite TV, beauty products, designer clothing and such comparable items as 'essentials'. It is important to have food to eat and clothes to wear, as well as a house to stay in. There are essentials for every family but particularly if you are living in Western society, where affluence is commonplace, we must be quick to examine our hearts regarding our attitudes towards the things that we spend. This is not primarily in order that we avoid overspending (though that is a valid point here) but also simply as stewards of what may be 'great riches/wealth' and how we use what God has given to us for the Glory of His Name.

4. What should our attitude be to 'luxury spending'?

Assuming we have established what luxury spending is (see above), then it is good to be realistic. For example, I might say to Binglin as she prepares to buy a beauty product, *'No! That's luxury spending. We must give that to the church!'* This can very quickly go from being right and Biblical to self-righteous and unloving. There are instances where a husband and wife can express their love to each other both in terms of gifts and also in agreeing certain luxuries that can be spent. I believe it is important for recreation and also for the good of a relationship for money to be spent on a date involving a restaurant meal and watching a film in a cinema. However, there are a few qualification sub-questions, which can act as a safeguard against unwise or overspending in this area:

a. Is it or does it have the potential to be a danger to your soul?

Do you *need* to go the gym and buy all the supplements to have the 'perfect body'? Do you *need* all the sports channels because you can't miss any big games? In such cases, such spending becomes idolatry.

b. Is this something I really like or enjoy or could 'do without it'?

Often over-spending and debt can be created by indulging in purchasing a number of things that are not even of great interest. For example, you may spend money on some kit or apparatus for athletics because you really enjoy it and do it competitively, but then do you also need to be buying products for other sports that you rarely play? This sub-question can be a good way of measuring and being more self-controlled.

c. What are the positive things about it?

This is difficult, but can help you to think not only about your spending, but how you use your time. I would suggest that luxury spending that may have some impact on you being well rested could be beneficial. It can certainly be more positive if it has some positive impact on your marriage. For example, if you both join a class or a club together.

You are maybe reading this section and thinking, 'We're nearly broke. Luxury spending is not an option.' If you are struggling with prior debts due to student loans or previous financial mistakes then it can be very difficult. However, the Scripture is abundantly clear that money is not the source of your happiness. It can become a source of stress, but it needn't necessarily be. In my experience with Binglin, some of our happiest memories have involved times where no money has been spent. For example, if an evening date is too expensive, then go for a cheaper lunch menu on your day off. If a night outside is desirable, go somewhere free. We live on a beautiful planet. If we can cherish what matters, particularly when finances are hard, then this does not 'make all the problems go away', but it can realign the focus of our hearts upon who and what really matters.

As you consider these questions and sub-questions, they can be a helpful way to introduce or analyse how you plan and budget in your marriage. However, you may be reading this already facing the effects of financial burdens and wondering what to do. I would first humbly and realistically admit that I am not a financial advisor and though there is clear Biblical counsel on many matters that may contribute to this, it would sometimes be important to speak to professionals. I have personally had fellowship with professional Christian financial advisers and I believe that speaking with such as these, who openly proclaim a God-centred, God-glorifying focus on their counsel and professional support, would be beneficial to any couple, let alone those facing difficulties. It is also important to think about whether the financial issues in your marriage are the external issue of other internal, deeper issues to do with areas such as covered in the Chapters in this book. This book can only serve a purpose if it points a couple to the Scriptures which is what informs and guides our marriages. It is also why it is advisable for any Christian couple to be in communication with and accountable to an older Christian couple (particularly in their local church), to their church leadership for ongoing support and counsel in all areas of marriage, financial matters included.

8

PARENTING

THE FOCUS OF this book is to consider how couples can live together practically in a Bible-saturated, God-centred way. The very first command that God gives to man is to procreate (Genesis 1:28) and so it is worth giving brief practical consideration to family life and parenting within any given marriage in this Chapter.

Better marriage, better parenting
For the 'average Christian family' consisting of a father, mother and two children, after your relationship with God, what is the most important relationship in this family?

Is this an important question? Is it a bad question? Perhaps many would say that all relationships are important. The relationship of a husband to his wife, or a father to his child, a mother to her child, they are all equally important, right? I have also observed family dynamics where the relationship to the child is considered the most important because they are the most vulnerable and dependent in the family.

The topic of parenting is a very important one when studying Biblical marriage. In answer to the question, I would argue that the relationship between the husband and the wife is the most important earthly relationship in any 'average Christian family'. Does this belittle the importance of a parent's relationship to their child? Absolutely not. In fact, the stronger the relationship between the husband and wife and the more time invested in that relationship, the stronger the relationship will be with the children and the more effective the parenting of the children will become. Consider these important points:

1. The marriage relationship comes first and the responsibility is life-long

The Lord has instituted marriage, which is a blessed covenant relationship between a man and a woman who come together as 'one flesh'. It doesn't require my clever observation to state that this relationship comes before and thus results in any parent-child relationship. It is certainly true to state that the dynamics of a family will change when a couple has children, but that does not then alter or reduce the importance of that marriage relationship. A husband and wife are 'one flesh' for all of their earthly lives together. This is a life-long relationship where the husband and wife have a responsibility for each other. Parents, your relationship to your children will change, but your relationship towards each other does not. Review what the Scriptures say about marriage (consider the reflections in Chapter 1) and realise that this is not altered when children come along.

2. A stronger marriage makes for stronger parenting

This point has been formative in my own personal family reflections. Let me illustrate this point with a counter example:

> Harry was married to Mindy for three years before the Lord blessed them with a child. He cherished her, spent time with her and led her in their study of the Scriptures. However, when their little boy Tony was born, things changed. The time that had been spent with Mindy is now time devoted to their son.

This is not because they don't think their marriage is important, but because their role as parents is so important.

Let me make this very clear and husbands must reconcile the importance of this point. If you do not prioritise the relationship you have with your wife and your role as a husband first, then your marriage *and* your parenting will suffer. Time dedicated to your children at the expense of your spouse is counter-productive and will do a disservice to your children in their upbringing.

We have reflected on a number of areas in which the need to fight for your marriage becomes prevalent. The hectic nature of life is a practical barrier that can often squeeze out your time with God, and similarly with your spouse! Therefore, the weight of being the spiritual leader in a marriage means that a husband has a responsibility to *make* time for God and to *make* time for his wife. This is not an optional extra! Husbands, the more stressed and busy your wife is, the more time is needed to pray for her and be with her. The more hectic life is becoming, the more need there is for you to hold your wife in your arms, tell her you love her, tell her how beautiful she is. This is the woman that God has prepared for you. She is far more precious than jewels (Proverbs 31:10) and your role is to lovingly lead her, care for her and protect her. That is a heavy responsibility but what a blessing it is. Similarly, wives, be motivated to spend time with your husband even when you are tired and want to rest. It is good to think about spending time when the kids have gone to bed, or to take the opportunity for babysitters to spend a night away together. Be realistic, but be creative. This time invested will be of such benefit to your marriage and also to your children.

3. A strong marriage is a safe environment and great witness to your children

It is my prayer that as my son grows up he will see a clear picture of a man who models what it means to love and to cherish his wife, Biblically. What a blessing it is for young boys to grow up to see Biblical manhood displayed by their fathers. Likewise, for young girls to see Biblical womanhood displayed by their mothers. This point cannot be stressed enough because children are very impressionable and parents have a formative influence in their upbringing and life. In addition to this, how safe a child will be growing up in an environment where mum and dad love and care for each other!

A family for God
I passionately believe that the more I love and centre my life around God and His Word, the better a husband that makes me. I believe that this logic applies also regarding our children and this is the key point that we will unravel in this Chapter by looking at Deuteronomy 6:4-9,

> Hear, O Israel: The Lord our God, the Lord is one. You shall love the Lord your God with all your heart and with all your soul and with all your might. And these words that I command you today shall be on your heart. You shall teach them diligently to your children, and shall talk of them when you sit in your house, and when you walk by the way, and when you lie down, and when you rise. You shall bind them as a sign on your hand, and they shall be as frontlets between your eyes. You shall write them on the doorposts of your house and on your gates.

If it is not apparent from this book then it will be clear when you read Scripture that you are not made for the sake of your spouse or your children, but rather, for Almighty God. And here in Deuteronomy we are given a very clear command to love God. There is so much that can be stated about this glorious passage and if husbands, if parents, get *this* right, then what a glorious impact this will make not only in the family home but for the sake of the Kingdom of the Living God.

This command concerns loving God, the One whose Glory He will not yield to another (Isaiah 48:11), for He is the absolute expression of perfection, the holy, just, righteous, perfect God who cannot be compared to another, whose worth and being is infinite and eternal for He is self-existent, self-determined. In the face of our sinfulness and rebellion, God has graciously rescued His chosen people and we are being commanded to love *this* Great and Glorious God. This command is written in such a way to make it clear that this isn't a passing or fleeting thing, and this is not 'one of many' loves. Our love for God should be with our entire heart, soul and might, namely, that God has *the* place in our hearts for nobody and nothing can compare to Him. This means that we need to know this God, by feasting upon the Scriptures more and more, by devoting more time to Him in prayer, deepening in our affection, in our passion and consequently in our all-encompassing love for Him.

Unsurprisingly, much more could be unpacked on this point but please notice the logical flow of this passage. The ravaging, passionate love that you have for Almighty God is what you teach to your children, what you talk about day after day. This is why the Lord Jesus declares that *where your treasure is, there your heart is also* (Matthew 6:21). If you love God with all of your heart, then that is a love that will motivate how you live and how you speak. A child being brought up in an environment where God is their first and absolute heartfelt love is a beautiful thing. And this is what is clearly in view in Ephesians 6:1-4,

> Children, obey your parents in the Lord, for this is right. 'Honour your father and mother' (this is the first commandment with a promise), 'that it may go well with you and that you may live long in the land.' Fathers, do not provoke your children to anger, but bring them up in the discipline and instruction of the Lord.

In Ephesians 5, we see that husbands are to love their wives as Christ by 'washing' their bride with the Word (5:26) and this is notably different to the command given to fathers who are to discipline and instruct. In Ephesians 6:4, Paul uses the word *ektrephete* (bring them up) and this term literally means to 'take out from' in order to feed and nourish. There is an emphasis in this verse that the child is to be brought up in an environment and culture that is different and set apart from this world. This is built upon the foundation of a world value of absolute truth from the Scriptures. The passage in Deuteronomy is thus all the more striking because the command to love the Lord our God with all our heart, soul and strength is then followed with a command to teach this to your children literally in all areas of their upbringing. And please notice to whom this command is written. Fathers. To bring up their children in the discipline and instruction of the Lord.

Genesis 18:19,

> For I have chosen him, that he may command his children and his household after him to keep the way of the Lord by doing righteousness and justice, so that the Lord may bring to Abraham what he has promised him.

A man could say that he doesn't have the 'gift of teaching' but what we need to realise from Scripture is that men are commanded to do this. Men, if you are reading this as a man who is not called to lead a church, if you are a father then *you are* called to lead your family.

This is why we go back to an already stated and stressed point which is that we must know God. Know who He is, and know His Word, be a student of the Word that you may be a teacher of it. This is not a calling to be as eloquent as John MacArthur or be as visibly passionate as John Piper. However, this calling could literally be to a recent convert from a life of crime and addiction, who is simply but intentionally teaching from the Scriptures. If this is the case, it is important that such a man is in membership in a local church, himself being a disciple, equipped in his handling of the Word and spiritual growth.

Fathers, do not leave this for your pastor, Sunday school teacher or even the internet! Consider if your child was drowning (drowning in their sin) and you are standing there and you shout, 'Where's my pastor?' That would be ridiculous! It's your job to go down there to save your child. You are in a position that your pastor, your Sunday school teacher, anyone else is not in. You know your child, he/she is your child. You know them in a way no outsider can or does and you have a role that nobody else does. This is why Paul warns fathers not to provoke their children to anger, because how easy it could be for sinful fathers to do just that. No, we are told to bring them up in the 'discipline and instruction of the Lord', and so let us unpack these two points in greater detail.

1. Discipline

During my days as a secondary school teacher, my work particularly focussed on teaching children with behavioural difficulties. I learned much from this work and it saddened me to see a consistent pattern with many teenagers who fitted this 'bracket', namely, a distinct lack of parental discipline and instruction. We must understand that children do not grow up 'good' and then develop bad habits. We are all born with a fallen nature (Psalm 51:5) and do not need to be taught how to misbehave and to act sinfully. Therefore, the role of the parent is crucial in training, rebuking and disciplining a child. The alternative would be 'illegitimate children' (Hebrews 12:8) and sinful patterns can lead to all levels of nasty and evil actions rooted in a sinful heart.

We could then foolishly go the other way and think, 'Oh well, not going to bring any more wicked sinners into this world'. No, that would be an abuse and defiance of Scripture and rooted by selfish motives. Children are a heritage from the Lord, Psalm 127:3, but they need discipline. Consider a young child. He or she is not trained how to sin—he or she *is* sinful. Therefore, if we then sit back at whatever stage in our child's growth like Eli with his wicked sons in 1 Samuel 2:23 and ask, 'Why do you do such things?' then we obviously do not understand that our children are sinners and need discipline.

My son, Amos, has certainly mastered the art of telling me what he does and does not want to do, and at times he will respond to my instruction by saying, 'Don't want that' or 'Don't like that'. In response I simply say, 'This isn't about what you like, this is about doing what you're told'. And that's it. My authority as a father is not governed by the mood of my three year old son. Of course, I make decisions based on his interests, but he is not the authority to tell me what those interests are. I am that authority upon the authority of God's Word. As a child gets older, there will need to be more explanation and reason, but your authority does not then diminish at that stage.

Therefore, Godly discipline must be Biblically consistent and firm. A husband and wife must be clear and united about the rules of the house for their children, and in enforcing this with the children. Much of the lack of discipline with children is caused by an inability or unwillingness to be firm and consistent. Being clear to your children about what they are allowed to do and what they must not do, both in terms of 'every day rules' and in any given situation, and then consistently sticking to this is essential. I recall a conversation with a Christian mother of a Godly family explaining how this was applied in a particular situation with her younger daughter at the time. This mother had warned her daughter about her misbehaviour in the park where she was playing, and the mother warned the child that if she misbehaved again, then they would not go shopping afterwards. As soon as the mother said this, she regretted making such a threat, because the mother wanted to go shopping as well as her daughter! The daughter then misbehaved again and even though the mother wanted to retract her threat, she did not. It was crucial that she stuck to what she said by being firm and consistent in her words, and the enforcement of the consequence of the child's misbehaviour. This example highlights a crucial point. It can be so easy for a parent to tell a child that they must behave or they will be punished and then not carry this out. Such an approach is damaging to the authority of the parent and the development of the child. Children must know the boundaries set by the authority of their parents and these must be rooted in Godly principles and in love for the child. When the Lord disciplines us as His children, He does not do so like some irrationally angry parent who wants to make His children suffer! God cares so much for you and He is lovingly shaping and refining you, which involves discipline. This is what we must do as parents to our children.

Permit me to unpack this point in relation to my son. As a father, and together as parents we clearly set and state the boundaries and consequences for misbehaviour. If Amos does misbehave and sins, then he will face a certain punishment where he under-stands that this is the consequence of his action. As well as this, I will also crucially state that his actions do not simply upset me as a father, but that they displease God. I will also then stress to Amos that God is a Father who forgives and his need of Christ. Following this, we will pray together and I will give him a cuddle.

2. Instruction

Deuteronomy 6:7 give us a clear imperative regarding the impor-tance of the family gathering to study God's Word in worship and praise to Him. So the first question to ask fathers in par-ticular, Are you doing this? Are you taking the lead in gathering your wife and children together to study the Scriptures? I implore you to make this an absolute priority in your weekly, and ideally, daily routine. It is so important for husbands to invest time in the spiritual life of their wives in time they spend together as a couple, and this also applies in no uncertain terms with their children. As my son was developing in his early months grow-ing from toddler to child, his understanding and awareness was limited, but I deemed it essential to begin forming a pattern of family devotions. It became a good habit where Binglin and I would sit with Amos to read a children's Bible book, sometimes sing a Christian song and I would lead us in prayer together. In addition to catechising our children, this is a daily routine each morning.

If you are gathering together as a family then this is a good practice. However, this passage in Deuteronomy goes further. The next question that we must carefully consider—Do you love God? You may think, *'What an obvious question, of course I do, because I'm a Christian.'* Would this love, as described in Deu-teronomy 6, be visible to your family? Children are particularly impressionable and they will see very clearly the things that moti-vate you, those things that bring the sparkle in your eye. What do you love to talk about? What do you devote your time to? If you spend hours in front of the television and constantly love to talk about your car and your favourite car shows, then what impact will a short family devotional have when you suddenly 'do your little God bit' for the day? A family devotional should not be in isolation to the way that you live because the day in, day out life that you live as a disciple of Jesus Christ whose love is passionately for the Living God *will* be noticeable and impact the way that you live. I have had people warn me about the 'curse of being a pastor's kid' and such a comment and phrase is not helpful but the underlying point is to be wary of not practising what you preach and applying what you teach. Again, it is why the command in Deuteronomy to love the Lord your God with all your heart, mind, soul and strength gets into view that this parenting and the Christian life is not a 'part-time business'. No, God is our business. He is our desire. He is the purpose. He is the One to whom we give Glory and by whom we instruct our children.

How does that impact life? Let me give you another example from my family when we go to a church service. We expect Amos to be 'toileted' and settled before we begin the service. We expect him to sit quietly as he has been taught, and he has been trained to do this. No child does this easily or naturally. They must be trained. And the reason is because this is God's house. At a time such as this, for my son to see mummy and daddy treating this seriously, approaching this passionately, that is a good, right and God-glorifying time.

Consider also how to treat others. We don't say to Amos, 'Oh, you're a good boy, so be kind'. No, we instruct him to be kind and to share because we are bringing him up in the discipline and instruction of the Lord. We are nourishing our child with what is needed that he can flourish to maturity.

However, we must realise that we cannot save our children.

The ultimate purpose of parental discipline and instruction is 'of the Lord'. It is nice to have well-behaved children who 'look the part' when you go to church, but this is not the objective. The objective is to create a culture that is centred around this Great God and to challenge the hearts of young lives that are not right with Him. Ultimately, heart change is needed and no amount of excellent parenting can do this. However, Biblical parenting may be the means by which the Holy Spirit will convict this young soul that they must come to the Lord in repentance and saving faith in Jesus Christ. Thus, to 'grow up in a Christian home' is a blessed thing if it is just *that*. A Christian home is one that has God at the centre, where He is the desire and the passion of the heart.

And so Job in 1:5,

> And when the days of the feast had run their course, Job would send and consecrate them, and he would rise early in the morning and offer burnt offerings according to the number of them all. For Job said, 'It may be that my children have sinned, and cursed God in their hearts.' Thus Job did continually.

Are you praying for your children? Job got up and consecrated his children to the Lord early in the morning. He does this early, and he does this daily. There is no delay. How serious is this?

It must be stressed that although children are a blessing from the Lord, they are not a necessity for any married couple (for example, if a couple are unable to have children), just as much as having a spouse is not necessary for a single person. Let me stress again, in Christ, and only in Him, do we have absolute satisfaction and everlasting hope and joy.

Also, children are not a hindrance in any way to any married couple. One of the most beautiful bonds on this earth is that of a mother to her child. I have witnessed my wife carrying our two children as they grew in her womb and then the incomparable bond between mother and child in the early months of their lives on this earth. That is something that we all cherished greatly. As children develop and grow, the role of the parents will adapt and change but it is abundantly clear that God has given a father and a mother a significant role of stewardship in the life of the child. Every child is made by God and is for God, and it is my prayer that in every individual relationship within a family there will be an ultimate and absolute focus upon the Lord God Almighty.

I am deeply challenged by this as a husband and as a father. I recall hearing a Christian brother who recently got engaged to his girlfriend sharing a prayer point about what an extra responsibility and weight this was in the face of his sinfulness and weakness. Therefore, we remind ourselves of the grace of the Gospel and that we are not going to be or expected to be 'the perfect role model', but if the love we have for the One who is becomes more and more clear to our family then we give Glory to our God and we will be more effective in leading our family, our children, to know and understand this Great God. Joshua 24:15,

> And if it is evil in your eyes to serve the Lord, choose this day whom you will serve, whether the gods your fathers served in the region beyond the River, or the gods of the Amorites in whose land you dwell. But as for me and my house, we will serve the Lord.

9

CULTURE

DO THE SCRIPTURES dictate? Do you seek God? Do you seek God joyfully? These are the types of questions that are fundamentally important not simply in any given marriage but simply in life!

To be Bible-centred, God-centred, God-glorifying believers is a declaration that almost every professing believer would heartily agree with. And yet, there is so frequently a significant inconsistency with how that person, how that couple, lives their lives. Permit me to elaborate with real-life examples from professing believers active in their service to the Lord:

- We were serving in a healthy church but we moved from that area to another area in the city. There aren't any healthy churches around this area but we moved to be closer to my in-laws and because there are better schools in this area.

- We have thought about moving but we couldn't afford to live in the type of area we would like.

- I know he's not a Christian but he is very respectful of my faith and would never stop me going to church.

- We couldn't do that in this country.

There is a common theme running through these, and countless other examples. The motivation, the drive, the reasoning behind decisions and actions are based on something other than Scripture. Now, it is clear that God does work through circumstances, one's cultural parameters, through financial constraints and so on. However, there is a subtle but significant difference here. When a believer declares that 'Christ is Lord of my life, I live for God's Glory' then what this should look like is *this* desire, *this* purpose driving your every decision and direction.

But in response you may ask: What happens if you are short of money? What happens if it means a more difficult situation? What if it means an inferior school for your children to study?

The Apostle Paul addresses this very situation in Philippians 3:4-8,

> [...] though I myself have reason for confidence in the flesh also. If anyone else thinks he has reason for confidence in the flesh, I have more: circumcised on the eighth day, of the people of Israel, of the tribe of Benjamin, a Hebrew of Hebrews; as to the law, a Pharisee; as to zeal, a persecutor of the church; as to righteousness under the law, blameless. But whatever gain I had, I counted as loss for the sake of Christ. Indeed, I count everything as loss because of the surpassing worth of knowing Christ Jesus my Lord. For his sake I have suffered the loss of all things and count them as rubbish, in order that I may gain Christ.

Paul is a living testimony to these inspired words! He literally considered all things as loss, all things as rubbish because of Christ, in order that he might know Christ. In practice this means that added difficulty, persecution, imprisonment would not deter him or alter his actions ... he lives for Christ! It is true to say that circumstances changed his plans on occasions (Acts 16:6, 1 Thessalonians 3:1) but his consistent 'drive' was Christ!

This is a fairly clear teaching to see and understand in Scripture but it is immensely challenging in practice. It can become so easy and natural to allow 'other things' to influence and impact our decisions and directions in life, where many a believer will then try to argue that they are 'seeking God's will' or 'this is God's will'. However, God's will can be understood by reading and obeying what He has said! The Scriptures do not change and God will never contradict. Therefore, this final Chapter is the foundation for what every marriage should look like – a Biblical one. And thus, we come to unpack what and how a Biblical culture can be sought and lived out in any marriage.

Biblical culture

A number of weeks after I met Binglin, we began to communicate on a semi-regular basis which involved communication via text and social media. One day, Binglin informed me that she had been in the library working all day (as she was nearing the completion of her Masters degree) and she said that she had only eaten a sandwich during the daytime. In response I wrote that I had enjoyed a nice filling meal and I included a cheeky 'emoji'. I have since been informed that this response was not well received! What was the problem? I sent a response in an attempt to be light-hearted and to enjoy 'some banter' with Binglin. However, Binglin's expectation was that I would come to the library to bring her food as a way to show her care. My response was interpreted as being cold-hearted and uncaring—though this was not my intention.

In the months and years that have followed, we have learned how differently we think on a range of issues, food being a key one, often due to our very different cultural backgrounds and upbringings. For example, on a day-to-day basis, I am happy to eat food quickly at times to get on and do other things and yet for Binglin eating food is vitally important as is represented in Chinese culture where every celebration and occasion is centred around a meal. Another example is that I like to be organised and well-prepared and so I am often unsettled by spontaneity and surprises, whereas Binglin often loves when people 'drop in' unexpectedly and when something happens that she did not expect.

So is one right and one wrong? Or one more right than the other? These are serious questions based on real issues. It is often the case that real-life disputes between couples can appear quite comical on the outside, but as many can testify, they are not so comical when faced with them in our lives day by day. As Binglin and I worked through our initial differences and the added upset caused by our different cultural backgrounds, it became apparent to me how much a person is influenced by his or her culture. In many ways in which I had previously thought I was being Biblical in my life, this was in fact a British person's definition of Biblical in a British context. Now this issue raises a number of very interesting practical topics and the one that we are considering is in relation to marriage. For Binglin and me in our relationship, as with any other couple, it was crucial to openly study, talk and pray about how we seek to have a 'Biblical culture' in our relationship. This is not simply an issue confined to couples that are cross-cultural. I passionately believe that it is fundamentally important that every couple, even when they are dating, prayerfully seek to abide and live by the Scriptures and let the Word of God, let the desire to Glorify God, to magnify Christ be the 'culture' by which the relationship is defined and lived out.

Our culture 'redeemed'?

The vision in Revelation 7:9 is striking: 'After this I looked, and behold, a great multitude that no one could number, from every nation, from all tribes and peoples and languages, standing before the throne and before the Lamb'.

This is a beautiful picture of what awaits any and every person who has been saved by the blood of Jesus Christ. This is a picture where people from all sorts of cultures come together in worship. It has been an immense pleasure to minister God's Word in a number of very different cultural settings and to see the way by which people worship the Lord in African, Indian, Chinese and British cultures is a truly beautiful thing. There are such notable differences where the cultural imprint has positively impacted upon the glorious reason they are coming together—Jesus Christ.

We must stress and rejoice that this vision in Revelation directs the attention of the Christian to the reality that our destination, our home is not on this earth. Praise God, it is heaven! This is why we rejoice that our earthly marriages will end, because heaven will not be a time where an earthly married couple will despair at the what is no more, but together with all the other saints rejoice in what we now have in the perfect union with the bridegroom Jesus Christ. Therefore, the 'culture' of every individual and every married couple is rooted in Christ and in our heavenly destination regardless of nationality, language or anything else. Thus, Paul writes in Galatians 3:28, 'There is neither Jew nor Greek, there is neither slave nor free, there is no male and female, for you are all one in Christ Jesus.'

This verse does not dismiss my culture and language as a Scottish person who speaks English (yes, we Scots actually do!) but it identifies that these factors are secondary, and as we will see, complementary to the foundation of who we are and the fellowship we have with Jesus Christ. Therefore, there is a big difference between my declaration that I am a 'Scottish Christian' and 'I am a Christian who is Scottish'. My being Scottish does not impact upon my identity as a Christian, hence why Paul dismisses these on this basis in this verse. In addition, every culture on this planet is in a fallen state. It is thus true to state on one level, we are redeemed *from* our culture (see 1 Peter 1:17-19). Our culture, which is in rebellion against God—where so much of what happens is counter-Scriptural—is what we are redeemed from by the saving blood of Christ. This means that no matter where you are from, what you have done and what cultural influences you have, Christ redeems you *from* that.

However, it is also true to say that Christ redeems creation, and thus culture, by His saving blood. This is emphasised at the end of a beautiful section in Colossians 1:19-20: 'For in him all the fullness of God was pleased to dwell, and through him to reconcile to himself all things, whether on earth or in heaven, making peace by the blood of his cross.'

In this passage the redemption of a fallen creation by Christ's saving blood is revealed to us. This does not in any way infer a universal salvation, for the lost will be eternally damned in hell under the weight of God's righteous wrath. However, for the born again believer, Paul goes on to write about how one's redemption in Christ can and does impact our entire being including talking about marriage, work and how we live. Therefore, the saving blood of Christ in the life of the believer thus redeems the uniqueness of our culture because our Christian faith now impacts every aspect of our lives.

The vision of Revelation is a celebration of the unique differences of every individual coming together in Christ Jesus. In this glorious, eternally saving way, our culture is redeemed. And thus, the unique traits of cultures throughout the world become like a number of bright and beautiful colours that come together to make a spectacularly striking picture. I am thankful that even in cultures rooted in atheism without any hint of Gospel influence, that they are redeemed by Jesus Christ where the uniqueness of one's culture is now being refined and transformed.

This is an important foundational point for Christian couples in marriage. If you can imagine that you are renting a property for six months with your spouse with a view to moving into a house on a long-term basis. The preparation, the planning, the decision-making will be driven towards the long-term investment. This is at the very heart of a Biblical culture in marriage. Our chief end is Christ, He is our perfect bridegroom and heaven is the wedding banquet feast. How does this then apply to your earthly circumstances and cultural influences? As we will have realised in our marriages and with some of the points covered in this book, there are many practical stumbling blocks from establishing a 'Biblical culture' in our marriages. However, the issue in any given marriage, such as my cross-cultural marriage, is not because of different culture, language, upbringing, environment. The issue is sin. Sin is what makes marriages difficult. And Christ is the redeemer from our sin. Christ is the One who redeems a husband from the countryside who likes the outdoors as He is the One who redeems a wife from the city who likes her quiet nights in. Our differences can now be celebrated, not because marriage is easy but because we have One who declared,

Come to me, all who labour and are heavy laden, and I will give you rest. Take my yoke upon you, and learn from me, for I am gentle and lowly in heart, and you will find rest for your souls. For my yoke is easy, and my burden is light (Matthew 11:28-30).

Cultural comforts

As a married couple, or as a single person, what do you really enjoy doing? What would you almost 'hate' to give up? When the Lord Jesus saw the heart of the rich young man He told him to give up the lot (Luke 18:18-30). And the startling reality is that there are a number of conditional parameters upon how we live our lives as Christians, and this is more apparent when two sinful people come together in marriage. In a marriage where two people have different backgrounds, upbringings, perhaps culture and language, different hobbies, interests and much more, how do you reconcile this?

First, recognise that in your own heart you are battling against the old sinful self, which *naturally* desires to put 'self' at the centre of it all. As two forgiven sinners acknowledge this, not just in theory but actually before God and each other, it creates an environment by which you seek to battle against this. Permit me to share a hypothetical example:

Martin was born in America but his family originates from India. He grew up in a nominal Christian home and it is very important to him to look after his parents and stay close to them. He works for a company but has had a heart for reaching his culture with the Gospel. Martin's wife, Natalie, is from Canada but has lived in America since she was a teenager. She has a distant relationship with her parents who are not believers. Natalie is very keen to serve in the church but she also likes to go shopping and enjoys spending quite a lot of money on 'nice' things, which she certainly wouldn't give up without a fight!

In this sort of example, there is nothing which would appear 'out of the ordinary', and yet so many potential dangers could become stumbling blocks to their relationship being rooted in Scripture where a 'Biblical culture' is established. If, for example, Martin and Natalie's cultural backgrounds become the premise for 'what they must do', it already becomes a competitor with Scripture. Martin could say that his parents must stay with them because this is what is done in Asian culture. However, in Scripture, although it is important to understand and aim to interpret how to honour your parents (as well as caring for an elderly parent who is widowed perhaps), this cultural practice cannot be a condition on seeking to do what is Scriptural. Also, if Martin is beginning to prayerfully sense the Lord's leading in moving to his homeland to 'make disciples', this is something that requires much prayer, discussion and counsel from their local church. However, were Natalie to place the condition that she can't do this because she doesn't want to leave her homeland because there is so much 'nice stuff', this again can become a stumbling block and place a condition upon a potentially Biblical culture in marriage.

Count the cost
The practical counsel that is required in this instance is simple; count the cost. The Lord Jesus is direct and to the point in Mark 8:34, 'If anyone would come after me, let him deny himself and take up his cross and follow me.'

When you came to Christ, as you come to Christ this very day, is this the declaration of your heart? To deny yourself is to deny the old sinful self that is put to death when you put your faith in Jesus Christ. This also has the very clear implication that we are to deny everything, namely give up everything for the sake of our Lord. Is this not what Peter and the disciples did in following Christ? Is this not what the Apostle Paul declared in Philippians 3:8?

You may be tempted to think, *'Well, I'm no Apostle. I'm a fairly run of the mill person in a typical marriage.'* Let's think about a very 'run of the mill' character in Scripture. A woman called Ruth who was a foreign woman who certainly wouldn't have been considered 'pastor's wife' or 'church woman's worker' material. At the beginning of the Book of Ruth, she is given the opportunity to return to her homeland of Moab as opposed to going with her mother-in-law to Bethlehem. We read in Ruth 1:16-17,

> But Ruth said, 'Do not urge me to leave you or to return from following you. For where you go I will go, and where you lodge I will lodge. Your people shall be my people, and your God my God. Where you die I will die, and there will I be buried. May the Lord do so to me and more also if anything but death parts me from you.'

By this declaration, Ruth is effectively giving up the hope of a husband and children (Naomi has no sons and nobody to redeem the family name), her homeland, her language and culture and her gods. Ruth is giving up everything! Why? What is motivating, what is driving her? This goes way beyond any reasonable level of loyalty to a mother-in-law. But rather, this is a declaration that she makes of a commitment to, and a faith in, the Living God. Ruth is not getting carried away by the emotion of it all like many at a great, loud evangelistic rally with the flashing lights and smoke machines where hundreds come forward at the altar call. No. This is Ruth and her mother-in-law. It's a bitter deal, and a commitment to a woman who has been dealt with bitterly (Ruth 1:20).

True genuine faith in the Living God involves looking beyond any present suffering with whole-hearted trust. True faith in the Living God involves looking at the present pleasure and perks and declaring them as 'rubbish' compared to gaining Christ. This is the posture and the heart that seeks to be Biblical and I pray that this would be what every married couple does, ideally before getting married! Count the cost! The cost of what you are giving up, namely everything, for the sake of Christ. Count that cost practically in coming together in marriage. As we have seen in this book, married life is a rich blessing but it is hard. Therefore, sit down and talk with your spouse and examine the areas in your life, the things that you have that would be hard to let go of. Discuss the 'conditions' you have not simply in your marriage, but in your faith as a Christian. The Lord Jesus is clear: Deny yourself and take up your cross. That means that in your heart you put everything aside for the sake of Christ. Can you say that this is what drives you closer together with your spouse? This is the heart of Biblical marriage. This is what a Biblical culture in marriage looks like. This is the beautiful and glorious picture of two forgiven sinners coming together as 'one flesh' in the Name of, and for the sake of, Jesus Christ!

I recall a time during our engagement when I had been invited to preach in a church in a rural area in the North of Scotland with a view to becoming the pastor. Binglin had visited there and had seen how isolated it was, and that the extent of cultural familiarity for her was the local Chinese takeaway! She was still very young, didn't know much of Scottish culture at all and struggled with the Scottish accent. When we talked about this, she declared from her heart that she would go where the Lord called me and, therefore, where He called us. Even though circumstances closed that door, I saw in this young woman a heart that was driven not by a devotion to me primarily, but to Almighty God. This example from my wife is a visible picture of one who counted the cost and sought to live according to the Scriptures for the Glory of God and the furtherance of His Kingdom.

CONCLUSION

Do not be conformed to this world, but be transformed by the renewal of your mind, that by testing you may discern what is the will of God, what is good and acceptable and perfect.—Romans 12:2.

IF YOU CAN picture an escalator that is heading down and it is packed with many people. This is a picture of the world and everyone moving in a direction away from the Living God, which seems so natural and feels so right. What is going to happen to the sinner who repents, namely turns in the opposite direction, and believes? As you battle along the opposite direction that seems so unnatural to the world, you will inevitably rub people up the wrong way and experience struggle and bumps and bruises along the way.

This analogy is applicable in many areas of the Christian life and it may be a helpful picture for married couples. The Scriptures are not simply a helpful manual for married life, but the very life and breath and definition of it. We have explored a number of the practical challenges and battles that couples can face in marriage. The underlying purpose of this is to enable a deeper Biblical understanding of what God has ordained marriage to be. This is what we are fighting for as we battle against issues of expectation, blame, trust, sexual purity and lust, money, parenting, culture and likely much more.

As I have meditated about marriage in studying for and writing this book, it has been a joyful, challenging and humbling experience. I certainly feel inexperienced to write on such matters, but far more sobering than that is how inadequate an example I am of what a Godly husband should be. It can be very easy to 'paint the right picture' externally with friends, church family and in other groups. However, as we have considered extensively, in marriage there is nowhere to hide. I can declare to a fellow believer that I hardly know how sinful I am, but he may look at me and think that I look like a 'good Christian who shows maturity for acknowledging his sin'. But there is nothing wise about sin and it acts as a debilitating cancer to the soul and to the heart of any marriage. Where sin dictates, sinful consequence follows.

In Romans 12:2 the Apostle Paul implores us not to be conformed to the world. The life of the Christian is not in name only, but in practice. We are moving away from the world and towards Jesus Christ, and thus, being conformed to the will of our Great God. Marriage is God's will. Marriage is God's beautiful design. Marriage is a covenant between a man and a woman. Marriage is a visible picture of the unbreakable union that we have as the church with our bridegroom, Jesus Christ. This is what makes a study of marriage about far more than simply practical counsel to those who are married. It is a celebration for every Christian at any stage of something that God has instituted and something that Christ has redeemed. Therefore, we can give glory to God because although every marriage consists of two sinners coming together, it is a marriage of two sinners who are united by a Gracious God. All Glory, honour and praise be to Him. Amen.

www.ingramcontent.com/pod-product-compliance
Lightning Source LLC
Chambersburg PA
CBHW060358090426
42734CB00011B/2182